# Decorating
## for
# Good

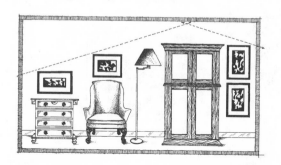

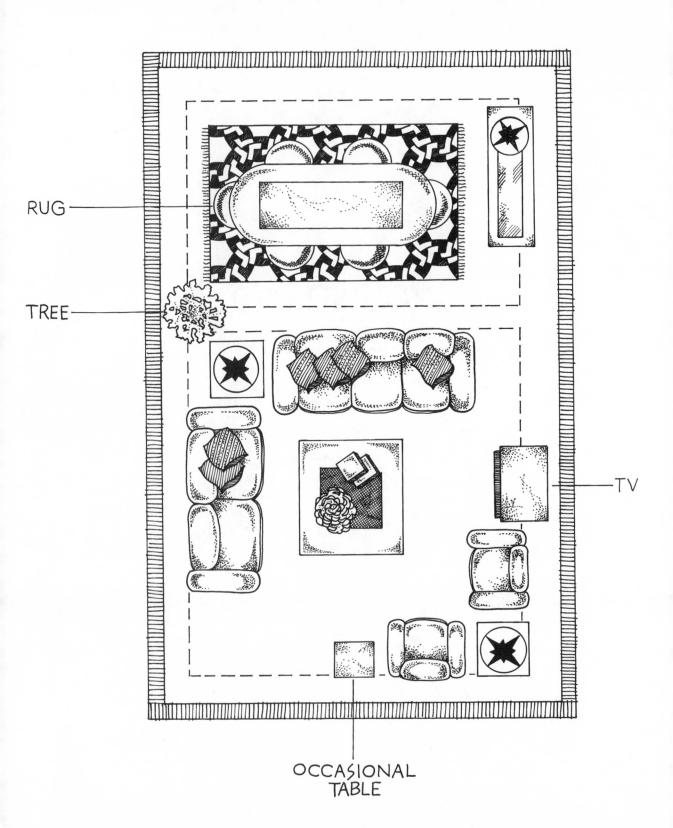

RUG

TREE

TV

OCCASIONAL
TABLE

*A Step-by-Step Guide to Rearranging*

*What You Already Own*

# Decorating
## for
# Good

**CAROLE TALBOTT**

Illustrations by CIRA COSENTINO     Text by MAGGIE MATTHEWS

CLARKSON POTTER/PUBLISHERS

NEW YORK

Published by Clarkson N. Potter, Inc., 201 East 50th Street, New York, New York 10022. Member of the Crown Publishing Group.

Random House, Inc. New York, Toronto, London, Sydney, Auckland
www.randomhouse.com

CLARKSON N. POTTER, POTTER, and colophon are registered trademarks of Random House, Inc.

Printed in the United States of America

Design by Lisa Sloane

Library of Congress Cataloging-in-Publication Data
Talbott, Carole.
    Decorating for Good : a step-by-step guide to rearranging what you already own / Carole Talbott : illustrations by Cira Cosentino : text by Maggie Matthews.—1st ed.
    (pbk.)
    1. Room layout (Dwellings)   2. House furnishings.   3. Interior decoration.   I. Matthews, Maggie, 1931– .   II. Title.
TX309.T35   1999
747—dc21                                                                98-55419
                                                                            CIP

ISBN 0-609-80371-9

10   9   8   7   6   5   4   3   2   1

First Edition

WITH LOVE, JUBILATION, AND GREAT PRIDE, *I dedicate this book to*

*Glenn Bryon Giles*

*Christopher Glenn Giles*

*Bryon Harrison Giles*

*Mary Ellen Giles*

# Acknowledgments

MY VERY SPECIAL THANKS to my family and dear friends. I will be forever grateful to all of you for breathing life into a gift that was waiting to be developed and shared.

Glenn Giles, my son, for giving reason, love, and support to my life every day of his.

Mary, my daughter-in-law, for organizing my life. Without her valiant efforts to take care of business, there would have been little or no time to write this book.

Don and Ellen Cooper, for returning health and pride to my life, and for teaching me the true meaning of friendship.

Jim and Pat House, for finally giving in and introducing me to national television. Most of all, I thank them for their unwavering support and constructive criticism.

Terry and Joy Keathley, for their acts of kindness and their giving spirit. Their faith in all things, especially me, is a constant reminder of God's work in progress.

Jerry Frankel and Richard Frankel, brothers for being supportive of a pioneer. I awaken each day remembering Jerry's words of wisdom: "Enjoy the climb—it is the best part of the journey." Richard's words, "You've really got something here," are a constant reminder that there is only one way to go: forward! Presenting this book to Jerry and Richard will be a shining moment in my life.

Billie Stresau, the *real* dear one!

Special thanks to my new best friends:

Maggie Matthews for her wonderful way with words and her editing skills. A great partner in adventure.

Cira Cosentino for her ability to bring line drawing to life. Her talent is a gift of the gods.

Heidi Rich for her amazing gift of gab and of gathering people together—the right people. A team player and a team maker.

And the wonderful group at Clarkson Potter: Kathryn Crosby, a source of true strength and guidance, John Son, Susan Westendorf, and Erin Bekowies.

Finally, I want to thank all the homeowners across the nation who were brave enough to turn their rooms over to a design-science-in-the-making, and all the certified Visual Coordinators around the world, who maintain the highest professional standards, guaranteeing complete satisfaction to the thousands of clients they are serving.

# Contents

**INTRODUCTION  11**

1. Visual Coordinations: A Step-by-Step Guide to Decorating Success  20

2. Breaking Down the Room  32

3. Reading the Architecture  42

4. Placing the Furniture  56

5. Hanging the Art  91

6. Layering the Accessories  117

7. The Other Rooms—A Field Trip  131

8. The Natural Colors for You: Fabric and Paint  138

9. Taking the Formula Outdoors: Landscaping  144

10. The Visual Reality, in Conclusion  152

Visual Coordination for the Professional  158

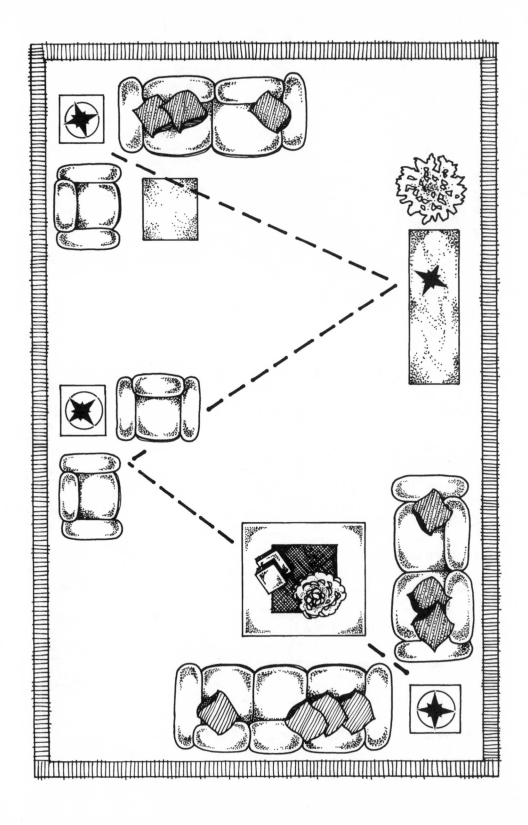

# Introduction

## WELCOME TO THE WORLD OF VISUAL COORDINATIONS

IMAGINE THIS. YOU CAN CHANGE YOUR HOME—adding beauty, comfort, connection, and renewal—simply by rearranging your furnishings. Sound too easy to be possible? Well, it's not. By following five simple steps, you can transform any space, from living rooms and bedrooms to hallways and patios.

Over the past fifteen years, as a decorator (or more precisely, a rearranger) and teacher, I have developed a clear and simple technique for rearranging the elements of your home—furniture, art, and accessories—according to your home's particular architectural design. This technique, called Visual Coordinations, will bring a fresh, renewed sense of vitality to every room of your home. Suddenly everything will be in its place, creating a beautiful, comfortable, harmonious environment. And the best thing is, it will cost you virtually nothing—because you already have everything you need!

The term "Visual Coordinations" perfectly marries the main concepts of my work. "Visual" refers to the aesthetic quality of the technique: creating beauty for the eye to behold. You don't need to be an artist or have a decorating background to understand the concepts—just an ability to see what feels beautiful to you. "Coordinations" refers to the harmonious functioning of parts that will turn every room of your house into a relaxed and balanced space. This book is the step-by-step guide that will get you there. "Coordinations" is also related to the word "coordinates"—a set of points or numbers that specify a location on a line, on a surface, or in space. Similarly, once you learn to see the major lines and shapes of your walls, floors, and ceilings, you'll be able to set your furnishings in their appropriate places.

Visual Coordinations will change the way you live. Your home will be more inviting and functional than it ever has been before. You can learn the technique simply by reading this book, see results in just a few hours, and apply it to any room of the house—even outside your house. The placement technique will always work; just use this book as a guide and an inspiration. There is nothing to fear and no possibility of failure!

The key to Visual Coordinations lies in the careful alignment of furniture, art, and accessories with the architectural shapes, lines, and features of a room. In other words, if you understand how a room is constructed, you'll be able to position any furnishings inside that

space in a way that complements the surrounding architecture. As you know, every room has certain architectural components: a floor, a ceiling, walls, and a door. It also contains other architectural features that can vary: windows, additional doors, steps, window seats, beams, built-ins. My placement technique shows you how to take all of these elements into consideration so that every piece has its proper place, creating a pleasing overall effect.

So many people make the critical mistake of ignoring the actual space of a room when they attempt to decorate. For example, instead of seeing two rectangular walls, a square floor, and a slanted ceiling encompassing a three-dimensional space, the new homeowner sees only a cold, empty room that needs to be filled. With that attitude, the result is usually a cluttered space, with the furniture functioning as filler. Since furniture can compete with the architecture if it isn't properly placed, a room, whether it contains fine antiques or modern furnishings, can end up looking out of balance and unattractive.

The foundation of a room—it's architectural elements—will rarely move (unless you knock down a wall), and so it is considered a constant. Items you can easily move around inside the room, including tables, chairs, mirrors, or lighting fixtures, are variables. Like a science, Visual Coordinations shows you how to unite the constant and the variables so that they work together, enhancing each other. Regardless of a room's structure, whether it has vaulted ceilings or sunken floors, this system will never fail because it works in accordance with the room, not against it.

And because the formula is based on a room's architecture, it can be applied to any space, including dens, kitchens, bedrooms, and even outdoor decks. Once you've identified the key architectural components of a room (which you'll learn about in Chapter 3), you'll begin to look at your home in a new way. That space in the living room corner will no longer look dead, but will become a vibrant, active part of the room. By understanding the placement technique, you'll learn to view the ceilings, floor, and walls, as well as the chairs, tables, and lamps, as dimensional forms. Once that is established, you'll discover the simple art of fitting the forms together, much like pieces of a puzzle, to create a beautiful room.

The greatest benefit of using this system is that you can achieve a stylish, comfortable room without spending a cent. This is because you use the furniture that you already own—the desk you worked at when you were in college, the end table that was given to you as a wedding gift, the rocking chair you found in your grandmother's attic. Pieces that are sentimental, antique, and cherished, or that you can't afford to replace, should not be hidden away in the basement just because you don't think they match the decor or, worse, because someone told you they were out of fashion. Chances are, the pieces don't look right because they don't fit into the room's composition—not because they are old-fashioned or unattractive. You deserve to feel proud of your belongings, especially ones that visitors will sit in, lean against, step on, and notice. With this placement technique, all your pieces will find their right place and look beautiful as a result.

Now, following a formula may sound daunting, especially if you think you're unfamiliar with architecture or don't consider yourself a visual person, but there's no need to fear. Over the past fifteen years I've fine-tuned Visual Coordinations and have successfully applied it to thousands of homes around the country, from one-bedroom apartments to grand estates. Having taught this system to hundreds of designers, retailers, and homeowners for almost six years, I have culled the easiest and most effective steps and have organized them into a practical guide. There is no jumping ahead, no thinking ahead, just a basic step-by-step system that will transform your room, your home, and your way of living. Insecurity, impatience, and costly mistakes will be things of the past. In their place will be feelings of pride, confidence, and satisfaction. Just think—in an afternoon you can have an inviting, beautiful home, one that you decorated yourself. What could feel better?

# The Evolution of Visual Coordinations

I remember visiting my grandmother's home as a little girl and noticing that her couch looked out of place. It seemed cramped and lifeless pushed up against the wall. Being a spunky little girl, as well as the apple of her eye, I was allowed to have my way, and my grandmother let me move the couch. This in turn led to my rearranging the chairs, the coffee table, and so on. My grandmother was so astonished and pleased with the results that she began spreading the word about my knack for rearranging to friends and neighbors.

Even with that early sign, I did not set out in life to develop the placement technique. I used my natural ability strictly as a hobby, helping friends, family, and neighbors to arrange their furnishings; it was easy for me and made me feel good that I was helping people enjoy their surroundings. Friends often encouraged me to turn it into a business, but I never imagined charging for my services until a difficult period hit and I needed to earn extra money. Somehow I convinced a local newspaper in Florida to do a story on my placement technique, and my career was on its way. Scattered articles in the press grew into cover stories and features in national magazines, including *Home*, *Redbook*, *Bride's*, and even *U.S. News & World Report*. Local television appearances became frequent guest spots on ABC's *The Home Show*. Eventually the ultimate boost came when I appeared on *Oprah*.

For the *Oprah* show, a panel of five designers, including me, the novice rearranger, demonstrated how we could redecorate a room on a $1,000 budget. I decided not to use a cent of the money, claiming I could make just as much of a difference without purchasing anything new. Needless to say, the producer was intrigued. The results were incredible.

# THE TWELVE MOST COMMON DECORATING DILEMMAS

Over the years, as I've listened to many of my students and clients describe their decorating dilemmas, I've noticed the same problems arise over and over. The following list describes these common stumbling blocks. If the underlying tone of frustration seems familiar, take heart. The problem can be solved.

1. I am always rearranging my furniture, but I never feel totally satisfied with the results.

2. I am tired of spending money and still not getting the look I want.

3. I would love to have professional help, but I'm afraid of what they would think of my things and what they would charge.

4. I don't have a creative bone in my body, so I just have to settle.

5. I know what I like, but I don't know how to put it all together.

6. I want my home to reflect my lifestyle, but how do you make trophies and family pictures look beautiful?

7. My home is too small to be beautiful.

The audience cheered enthusiastically at the way I transformed the room by simply rearranging the furniture that was already there. My phone lines were jammed for weeks.

Most callers wanted information on any training or how-to instruction I offered. They asked how I had learned to rearrange the furniture the way I had demonstrated on television. It became clear that I needed to spread my ideas and teach the placement technique. But instructing others meant that I had to provide solid, easy-to-follow steps backed by clear, rational information. My intuition alone

8. My home is too large to be warm and inviting.

9. I am moving into a new home, and I'm afraid that what I already have won't work there.

10. I want to recover the furniture or buy some new drapes, but fabrics are so confusing. I don't have a clue where to begin.

11. My home is well decorated, but it just doesn't feel comfortable.

12. I want to buy a new piece of furniture, but I'm so worried it won't match the rest of my things.

Of course the list goes on, but these are the central issues that plague most people who want to redecorate. You might find it hard to believe that so many negatives can be turned around with a simple formula, but they can. Visual Coordinations allows you to better understand your space, your belongings, and your decorating goals. It also eliminates the confusion that comes when you're about to make a purchase. By knowing exactly what you are looking for and where it will be placed in your home, confusion turns into confidence.

wouldn't do! So for several years, while I worked with clients, I analyzed my every move, figuring out exactly what made the placement technique work so well.

Eventually I realized that although the architectural style of the homes varied, as did the style of the furnishings, there was a constant component in every home I worked on—the pattern of placement. In this, my first book, I have outlined this placement technique, called Visual Coordinations, clearly and carefully, in order to give you the motivation, skills, and power to change the way you live. I hope you'll

trust in the technique, because I promise you will not be disappointed with the results.

Before closing this chapter, I'd like to tell you about the magnificent Imperial Gardens of Beijing. Reflecting an ancient and unique philosophy, these gardens are different from all others in the world.

Centuries ago, the Chinese emperors designed these gardens with elaborate groupings of plants and trees, while deliberately concealing parts of the temples and pavilions to create a feeling of discovery and oneness. Huge rocks are carefully positioned as abstract sculptures, emulating the art of nature. Pathways are set in graceful weaving patterns, slowly revealing delicate treasures that beckon one to explore at one's leisure. Curves add a diversity of views and points of interest to the journey. It is important that visitors to the gardens feel a part of this masterpiece of nature. Ironically, the discipline of this natural order creates a wonderful sense of freedom. Ask anyone who has been there.

To me, the Imperial Gardens of Beijing display an innate beauty and sense of pride, with a strong element of repose that invites you to relax and recharge. The emperors wanted to create a retreat that inspired a reverence for nature. I was astonished to discover the similarities between these ancient traditions and the effect that Visual Coordinations is meant to achieve. Like the Imperial Gardens of Beijing, Visual Coordinations leaves you with a sense of pride in your home, a greater appreciation for the things you have, and pleasure in the renewed beauty and comfort of your surroundings. It also turns your home into a retreat, a place where you can relax and recharge your energies.

# 1

# Visual Coordinations: A Step-by-Step Guide to Decorating Success

I like to think of Visual Coordinations as a creative science—a breakthrough method of turning the creative process into a simple, accurate science, guaranteed to succeed. The first step in making the technique work for you is to trust it. In order to do that, you need to forget every other decorating rule, method, or tip you've heard or read. Visual Coordinations will force you to think in a completely new and different way about your belongings, your rooms, and your entire home. Go with it—you'll be amazed at what a difference it will make.

In order to train your mind to think in a new way, you have to clear it, setting aside any preconceived notions—the first request I make of my students. When our minds are uncluttered, we can absorb much more—like a sponge that soaks up more water after it is properly wrung out. By clearing your mind, you also set loose any fear, insecurity, or reluctance you may have about rearranging your room. After all, you've gone to the trouble of opening this book, so you might as well complete the project and see what happens.

As you read through this book and start to move your furnishings, try not to jump ahead; stay focused on the task at hand. If you follow the steps as I have set them, you will have no problems in achieving success—comfortable and beautiful rooms—but if you're tempted to skip a step, you may waste time and become frustrated.

As you probably know, the right side of the brain is used for analysis, reasoning, and calculations, while the left side controls imagination and creativity. Numerous studies have examined the differences in the sides, and exercises have been created to stimulate certain functions of each. If you've ever taken an art course or a creative-writing class, you may have learned about using more of the left side of your brain. Visual Coordinations is not designed as a brain test, but it will teach you how to think visually. As you learn to use the process, you may notice a shift in your perception.

Although people carry different levels of ability, everyone wants to be more creative. Creativity marks our individuality and keeps new inspirations pouring into our lives. Even if you do not consider yourself a creative person, Visual Coordinations allows you to express the creativity you do have. You use the furnishings that you already own, rather than relying on a professional to choose a fashionable upholstery fabric or suggest a sofa style. Those chairs, light fixtures, bookends, and mirrors live in your home because you brought them in— most likely in a way that was meaningful to you. You may not have purchased them all; maybe they were passed down from generation to generation, or given to you as a gift, but the thing to remember is that they belong to *you* and mark your style. As soon as a guest walks into your home, he sees and senses your style from these furnishings.

If you are unhappy with some of your furnishings but worry that you're not creative enough to choose a piece that would work well in your space, Visual Coordinations will help you. This is where the science of my placement technique takes over. Visual Coordinations is devised as a solid set of steps with specific guidelines that have been tested thousands of times. The steps will work for anyone, regardless of background, education, or creative ability. By precisely aligning your furniture with the architecture, you will immediately discover what areas of the room need furnishing, the appropriate size of the furnishing, and its function. Once you have this information, it will be much easier to walk into a store and confidently make a purchase.

## Think Jigsaw Puzzle

Since the Visual Coordinations formula trains you to think in new ways, you will start to see your living space as you never have before. One way my students stay focused on the formula during this mental transition is to imagine the room as a jigsaw puzzle. Your furniture, art, and accessories represent puzzle pieces of varying shapes, sizes, and colors. The pieces make no sense when they are thrown together in a box or on a tabletop, just as your furniture looks awkward if it is poorly positioned in a room. You have to meticulously fit together each piece of the puzzle—sofa, table, lamp—in order to create a comfortable, beautiful, and balanced room. There is no way to successfully complete a puzzle unless every piece fits together perfectly; likewise, if you do not follow the steps as I have outlined them,

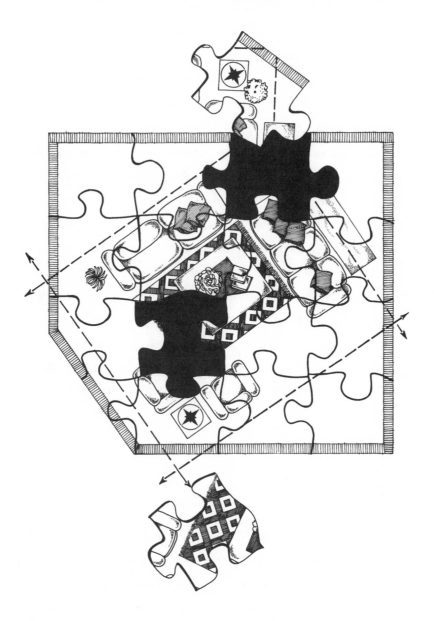

the space will not turn into the complete, livable room you want.

Doing a jigsaw puzzle forces you to focus on the shape of each piece and to observe how its contours will complement the surrounding ones. Look at your furniture in the same way, forgetting its function. Instead of viewing a chair as a place to sit, see it strictly as a shape. This concept will apply to every piece of furniture, art, or accessory in the room, so you can ask yourself if the chair, table, and lamp are vertical, horizontal, or diagonal; square, round, or oblong; thin or wide, tall or short. If you think of that lounge chair as a horizontal rectangle instead of a comfy place to curl up and relax, you're on the right track.

Reading shapes is one of the earliest skills we learn as children; it is how we first became acquainted with the world around us. Try to revert (somewhat) to your childhood as you re-look at your room. It will help you understand this totally new approach to decorating, as well as making the whole process of redecorating easier and more fun. Otherwise ordinary objects, such as books or tables, take on new significance and become multidimensional forms with edges, angles, and weight. Therefore, when you add a chair to a room, you will not be mired down in the notion that it is an object used for sitting, but rather, you can think of it as a spatial form that should be placed according to the architectural lines of the room and the other furnishings.

## Five Steps to Success

Visual Coordinations is carefully organized, making it important to follow each step in the order in which it is presented to achieve the most comfortable and creative use of your space. Completing the process in this way allows it to work perfectly in every situation. Here is an overview of the Visual Coordinations steps. They will be discussed in more detail in the following chapters.

1. BREAKING DOWN THE ROOM — PREPARING THE ROOM FOR THE DECORATING FORMULA

2. READING THE ARCHITECTURE — ANALYZING THE LINES AND STRUCTURE OF THE ROOM

3. POSITIONING YOUR FURNITURE — PLACING CHAIRS, TABLES, AND SOFAS IN ALIGNMENT WITH THE ARCHITECTURE

4. POSITIONING YOUR ART — HANGING ITEMS ON THE WALLS

5. POSITIONING YOUR ACCESSORIES — APPLYING THE FINISHING TOUCHES WITH BOOKS, COLLECTIONS, PLANTS, AND KNICKKNACKS

Staying focused on performing one step at a time can be difficult; we all have the tendency to jump ahead and worry about the next task. Since it is integral to the placement system to stay on track, I often tell my students to picture a tree to help them stay focused.

The tree is a great representation of Visual Coordinations. The method is organic; it provides a systematic coordination of parts. By arranging your furnishings in their proper alignment, you're trying to attain the natural order of your home. It is this balance and order that lead to both beauty and comfort.

A tree also grows and changes, adapting to the seasons and to its surroundings. Visual Coordinations works in any room and in any home. You do not have to worry about replacing furnishings or adding new ones; the system adapts to suit your needs and the furniture you already own.

Finally, a tree is made up of distinct parts, just as Visual Coordinations has distinct steps. The tree is composed of roots, a trunk, branches, and leaves. These parts work together and rely on each other. Just as branches cannot grow from roots, nor leaves grow out of a trunk, you cannot accomplish the second step of the placement technique without tackling the first.

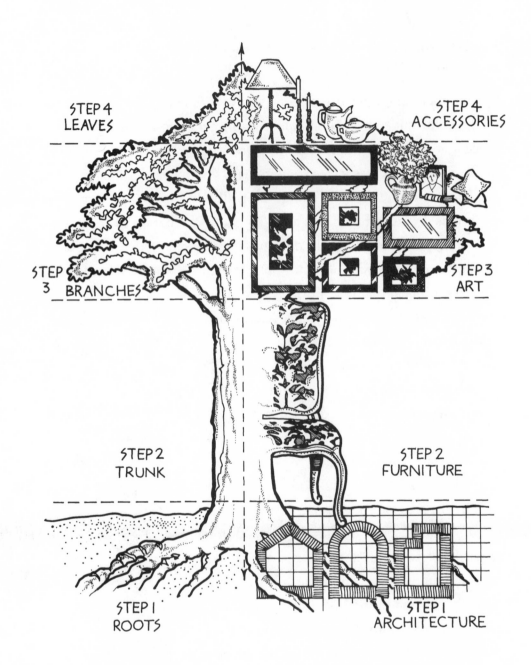

STEP 4
LEAVES

STEP 4
ACCESSORIES

STEP
3
BRANCHES

STEP 3
ART

STEP 2
TRUNK

STEP 2
FURNITURE

STEP 1
ROOTS

STEP 1
ARCHITECTURE

SOIL = ROOM PREP — Think of breaking down the room as clearing the area before planting. You are preparing the soil for the creation of something wonderful.

ROOTS = ARCHITECTURE (STEP 1) — The roots are the foundation of the tree, and the architecture defines the character of a home. Once you establish the type of architecture your room represents, you can begin the rearranging process.

TRUNK = FURNITURE (STEP 2) — The growth of the trunk out of the roots parallels the placement of the furniture according to the architecture. Without a trunk, nothing supports the tree; similarly, the architecture supports the placement of your furniture.

BRANCHES = ART (STEP 3) — After the trunk is firmly established, it forms an identity by extending outward with branches. The same thing happens with your room. Once you have correctly aligned the furniture with the architecture, you can add and layer art, extending the room's visual impact. If you attempt to position art before placing the furniture, you will destroy the natural order of the room and will not be able to find the right placement points for the art. That's why it is so important to complete each step before moving on to the next one.

LEAVES = ACCESSORIES (STEP 4) — The final component of the tree is its leaves, the last step in the growth process. Leaves add color and distinguish one tree from the next. Accessories tell visitors to your home who you are and what you like. They highlight your color sense, your design sense, and your personality. Just as leaves change with the seasons, the small movable objects in your home are also likely to change from time to time. You might pick up a little bowl at an antique store, receive a bud vase as a thank-you gift, bring out holiday figurines for the season, or just move a pair of candlesticks from the living room to the dining room.

# Checkpoints: Your Safety Net

Now that you're getting a clearer idea of what to expect with the Visual Coordinations steps, you may be wondering how you'll know if the method is working. We all fear trying something new and worry about getting the results we intend. To reassure you, the placement technique has built-in checkpoints to keep you on track.

As you're working through the Visual Coordinations steps, even while you're breaking down the room, you'll probably sense a difference in your living space. You'll notice new parts of the room and rediscover beauty in your objects. Along with the excitement of knowing you are transforming your home, you can also look for signs that you are following the steps correctly—these are the checkpoints I will refer to throughout the book.

## 1. PEAKS AND VALLEYS

Peaks and valleys exist in many forms throughout nature, and there is no reason why they cannot exist inside your home as well. Peaks, of course, represent height, while valleys represent low areas. The same is true in decorating, but peaks can also mean volume and weight, while valleys provide pause or rest, an opportunity to breathe and appreciate the surroundings. Peaks and valleys give rooms a sense of life, balance, and movement.

Every object in a room can represent a peak or a valley, depending on its size, structure, and placement. Do not feel that because a piece is small, such as a paperweight, it must be a valley. You can extend the

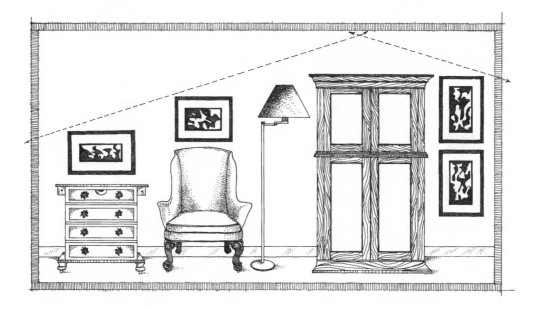

shape or height of any object by stacking, clustering, or layering. In this case, a paperweight looks great on top of a stack of coffee-table books, where it can sit high up in a peak position. Every peak is grounded by a strong bottom weight, such as a major piece of furniture. Once you've established this weight, you can add layers to extend the shape and add height. You can add layers with art, accessories, or potted trees and other tall forms. Valleys are the dips or pauses in placement. They give you a chance to breathe and to take a moment to appreciate your efforts.

It doesn't matter which role a piece plays, as long as it's counter balanced. Peaks and valleys should happen all over a room—against the walls, on top of a side table, occasionally in a corner—so make sure you're not focusing on only one part of the room. Also, consider the connection between groups of objects in your home. If most of the objects in your living room are pieces of heavy furniture, chances are the space feels stiff and uninviting. You can layer some smaller, lighter pieces to raise the room's spirit.

After all, it's much more interesting to walk into a room that feels alive and fluid. Peaks and valleys ensure that a room looks balanced and beautiful, but also active and exciting, showing that someone actually uses it. Once you start moving your furnishings, notice how the ups and downs of peaks and valleys dramatically affect the mood of a room, re-energizing the entire space.

## 2. WEAVING TRAFFIC PATTERN

Placing major furniture pieces away from the walls and bringing them out into the room forces you to weave your way through the room, instead of shooting straight through. It allows you and your guests to notice and appreciate the contents of the room more closely. It also promotes sociability (which I will discuss later) because the chairs and sofa are in closer proximity to each other. Keep in mind that you do not live in a waiting room. Of course you have to avoid creating an

obstacle by pulling the furnishings toward the center. Totally incorrect to this system!

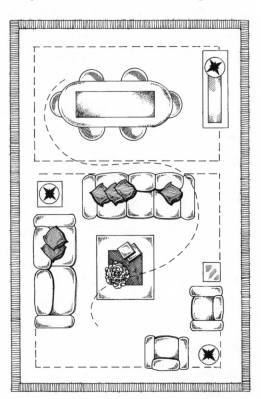

Weaving traffic patterns are subtle and sensually comforting, drawing you into and through a room, connecting you to your surroundings. Like peaks and valleys, weaving traffic patterns help us to emulate the loose, flowing motions of nature, creating freedom and comfort in the home. After all, we enter a room to live *in* it, not around it.

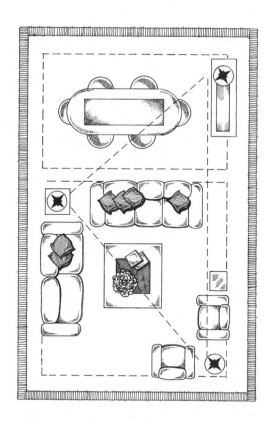

## 3. DIAGONAL OR TRIANGULAR LIGHTING

This third checkpoint will automatically work if you have followed the Visual Coordinations system step by step and if you are aware of the first two checkpoints. If you have achieved peaks and valleys, and especially if you have a weaving traffic pattern in your room, your lighting will fall into a diagonal or triangular pattern—leaving no dark corners or overly bright conversation areas.

Lighting can really change the mood of a room, but it is often overlooked during redecorating. Most people rely on various lamps or overhead lights for complete satisfaction. The Visual Coordinations technique asks you to look closely at your light sources and make sure that they connect with the overall composition of your furniture placement.

Lamps, standing lights, chandeliers, and other movable light sources are considered a part of your furnishings. They should be placed according to their size, shape, and weight in proper alignment with your room's architecture and furnishings. If the system is followed correctly, a diagonal or triangular lighting pattern should emerge automatically. Light will overlap as it falls across the room, thereby creating a gradation in intensity without any spotlights.

# 2

# Breaking Down the Room

Now that you understand the Visual Coordinations system, I hope you are excited and ready to begin. There are a few things to consider in preparing your room for the rearranging. Although undertaking the process will be an exhilarating experience that should take only a few hours, I suggest you set aside the entire day. Choose a time when you are feeling well rested and can stay focused, and when you can work through the formula without interruption. Weekends are usually the most convenient, and extra muscle is more likely to be available then. It is also a good idea to start small—tackle one room at a time instead of the whole house, letting your motivation get a strong hold.

# Get Help

Some steps of the process require you to move furniture. If your tables, sofas, or other pieces are very heavy, please do not attempt to move them yourself. Rearranging your furniture is not worth a strained back or sore legs. Instead, enlist friends, family, or neighbors to help you. You'll probably need help only for the initial break-down and for resituating the furniture, so estimate at most one hour of their time. If your assistants are having too much fun to leave, there are plenty of ways they can make the process move more quickly—breaking down the room's smaller pieces and then putting them in their new places, hanging art, even helping with the accessories. Also, keep in mind that moving cautiously and lifting with your lower body will mean a happy ending to the day.

If some of your furniture is too heavy or unwieldy for the non-professional to move, secure the services of a moving company in advance. Plan for them to arrive about two hours after you start breaking down the room. As with your friends and neighbors, movers will be able to complete their job in about one hour. The cost factor of using a professional is minimal, while the risk factor of injury to you or your inexperienced helpers is not.

# Dress the Part

Remember that you'll be moving furniture, hanging art, and perhaps doing some under-the-carpet cleaning while you're at it. Make sure you and any helpers are dressed in comfortable clothing that enables you to move freely and step firmly. Leggings, T-shirts, and rubber-soled shoes should be the uniform of the day. Jewelry, belts, loops, or anything that can grab or scratch is a definite no-no.

# Tools of the Trade

Being prepared is vital to any smooth-running project. Think of the times you've been focused and immersed in a job, only to have to stop and look for tools—not only a time-waster, but frustrating too. Many of the tools you'll need are common household items, but if you don't have them all, borrow or buy them before you begin the job. If you are moving into a new home, you'll probably require additional items.

- ❖ Screwdriver—for removing wall mounts
- ❖ Pliers—for easy removal of picture hooks
- ❖ Spackling compound—for patching holes caused by picture hooks
- ❖ Putty knife—for applying spackling
- ❖ Picture hooks—be sure to have a variety of new ones on hand: 20-, 30-, 50-, and 100-lb. sizes.
- ❖ Hammer and nails—for hanging art
- ❖ Ladder—for hanging art
- ❖ Tape measure—for positioning art
- ❖ Touch-up paint—to cover spackling

# Photographing Your Room

Sometimes, after you've finished a project—especially one that involves improving an object or a space—you forget what it looked like before you started. Aside from having a beautiful room when you're done, it can be difficult to measure how much of your hard work was a success. To get a better idea of how you're improving the room, I suggest that you take photographs before you begin, during the process, and of course after you've achieved the look you want. Photos allow you to share the transformation with family and friends, providing interesting conversation material and documentation of your success. Plus, showing them off also gives you a well-deserved surge of pride.

Here are some simple tips that I devised after observing many professional photographers on shoots for magazines or newspapers. Often, upon returning to photograph a finished room, they would stand bewildered, wondering where they had shot from before.

❖ As you look through the lens, establish a consistent height—or top edge—to each frame. I use the top of a window, door frame, or architectural ledge. Maintaining that same height in all the photos will keep your frames the same from top to bottom. Next, shoot diagonally across the room, corner to corner, taking four separate shots. This will cover the entire space of each room.

❖ Mark the exact spot where you're standing when you shoot so that your "before" and "after" shots are comparable. This may seem unnecessary, but your room's transformation will be so dramatic that you may not remember where you were standing before. Use masking tape, which will not cause any damage and can be easily removed.

❖ I also recommend taking "before" and "after" shots of all tabletops and shelves. That way, you can refer to a complete series. As an added benefit, these photos create an instant album for insur- ance purposes—a task many of us don't think of, or keep postponing, due to our busy lives.

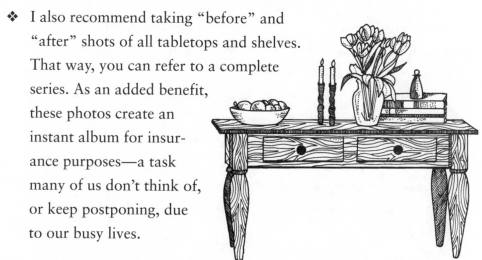

# FLOOR PLANS: ARE THEY REALLY NECESSARY?

If you keep in mind that Visual Coordinations is like working a puzzle in three dimensions, you'll realize that floor plans are not necessary for successfully redecorating a space. Many people are tempted to use floor plans when they redecorate because it gives them the exact dimensions of a space. Unfortunately, they forget that this "space" is as flat as the piece of paper on which the plan is drawn.

With Visual Coordinations, you learn how to build your perception, creative capacities, and problem-solving skills by looking at a room as a whole, and *then* figuring out how the pieces, such as furniture and accessories, fit into it. Working in the actual room, rather than on paper, gives you a sense of space, scale, and volume all at once. It frees you from relying on the paper model and forces you to be physically within the process. My theory is that you have to be *in* a space to make it work. Floor plans do not allow you to feel the room as you're making decisions and placing objects. Looking at a floor plan, for example, you might decide to place your largest piece of furniture against the longest wall, in order to fill up the wall space. With Visual Coordinations, on the other hand, you'll be able to see that either the couch or the piano has the weight, volume, and shape to fill up that wall space, or that they might work better elsewhere in the room, according to the architectural lines and focal point. In addition, you'll learn that some furniture works best pulled away from the wall, something you can't see in a floor plan.

I always ask my seminar students to make "before" and "after" floor plans during their training, just to prove they don't work. Old habits are sometimes hard to break, though, so if drawing the furniture placement in your room will help you in some way, go ahead. For the purpose of rearranging, you only need to draw the major pieces of furniture, both before and after. And since it's for your eyes only, don't worry about drawing to exact scale.

# Breaking Down the Room

You and your helpers are dressed comfortably. The tools are conveniently placed nearby. Refreshments are on hand for a lunch or snack break. You've taken a few snapshots of the room. Your calendar is clear for the next few hours. Well then, the room awaits its transformation! Let's begin by breaking it down.

The first step in the process is to remove virtually everything from the room. You'll want to store your furnishings temporarily in a holding area, so make sure you have access to a clear space in a nearby room or hallway for the furniture, and a kitchen countertop or dining room table for the small items. Start with the accessories, then remove the art, and finally move out as much of the furniture as possible. When you're done, only the largest, heaviest, and most cumbersome items should remain. These pieces do not necessarily have to be removed; you can push them to the side or to the center of the room. The key is for you to be able to clearly focus on the room's architectural details, without any distractions or obstacles.

For all you chronic rearrangers, please note that breaking down the room is the biggest time-saver of all, as well as the key to a successful transformation. Most people make the mistake of rearranging small areas at a time, or moving a few things here and there, with no overall plan in mind. In order to give your room a fresh new style, you *must* clear it—and your mind—completely, forgetting the way the space looked before you started.

Starting with a clean slate makes the entire process much smoother and easier. Here are a few easy steps to make it quick and effortless:

37

# THE STEP-BY-STEP BREAKDOWN

1. Remove all accessories—all items sitting on or in a piece of furniture. As you move them to the holding area, group all like items together, such as lamps, plants, books, pillows, candlesticks, framed photos, and figurines. By making the items easy to find, you save time when you're ready to reaccessorize the room.

2. Remove all art from the walls and group according to style, shape, and size. Hallways make a perfect holding area for art. This is also the time to remove picture hooks and then spackle the holes and touch up with a little paint.

3. Be sure to unplug all wiring to lamps and electronic devices. Use colored tape or dot stickers to code the wires and connections for sound equipment. (As you pull one wire out, put a red dot on the wire and another on the corresponding receptacle. For the next wire and receptacle, use green dots, and so on. Each wire and its receptacle can then be identified by their color.)

4. Remove shelves from display cabinets, starting with the bottom shelf and working up. (When it's time to replace the shelves, start with the top one and work down.) This drastically reduces the risk of damage while moving, unloading, and reloading the cabinet.

5. Remove all furniture that you and your helpers can easily transfer to the holding area. As I mentioned before, anything that is too heavy to remove can be pushed to one side of the room. Now you have an (almost) empty room. Just as an artist starts with a clear canvas, you start with a clear room in which you can easily read the architectural features and start having some real fun.

Although moving every item out of your room sounds daunting, you'll be surprised at how little time it actually takes. Go at your own pace, though, especially if you're tackling this step without a helper. There's no rush. And don't worry about the mess you may be making in other rooms in the process. In a few more steps, you'll have everything in its place. Just be patient and keep trusting the technique.

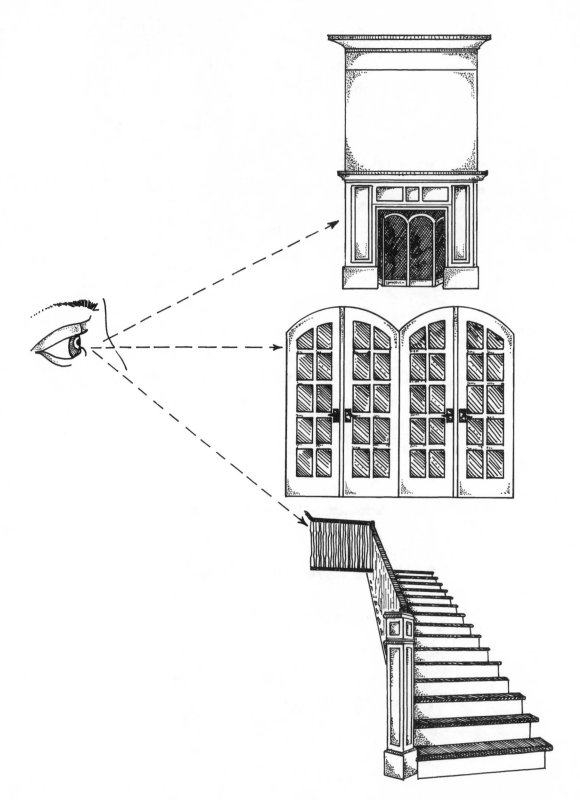

# Determining the Focal Point

Now that the room is clear, you can look at it in a totally different way, without any distractions. For all the hours you've spent in here, you've probably given little, if any, thought to the *architectural* focal point of the room. You're probably familiar with the use of "focal point" to mean a specific item that is featured and on which all eyes immediately fall upon entering a room. In many cases this tends to be the television, a piano, a sculpture, or a dramatic wall hanging. When I refer to architectural focal points, however, I mean a part of the structure or architecture of the room. This is the first and most important difference between Visual Coordinations and more traditional design theories.

The easiest way to determine the architectural focal point is to identify the feature that attracts your attention. Let your eye naturally lead you to it. Some examples of common focal points are windows, fireplaces, built-in wall units, arches, stairways, and even a wall if it is large or bare. Of course a room can have several focal points, but there will always be one feature that is the strongest; this is the point you should use. Also, furniture, if it is fixed—attached to a wall, like a built-in bookcase, for example—can become a focal point because it is part of the room's structure.

It is important to determine the architectural focal point because you work from that point to connect the contents of the room to its structure. *The focal point becomes the central axis on which the room balances.*

# 3

# Reading the Architecture

Once you have completely broken down the room and selected the architectural focal point, you're ready to identify the shape and lines of the room. While this may sound a bit confusing, it's actually a simple step that will guide you through the rearranging process. Think of the architecture as a support system that contains the belongings you are about to arrange.

Remember our analogy of the tree? We are starting at the roots. The architecture is firmly set and supports the beauty about to unfold.

How often do you walk into a room and consider its architecture? Most of us look beyond that to appraise the view, judge the size of the space, or decide whether it will accommodate certain pieces of furniture. We usually look at the space in its entirety, instead of breaking it down into shapes and lines, to determine the room's architectural features. Until now, there hasn't been a logical reason to look at a room in any other way, but this is the time to change your viewpoint forever.

When reading the architecture, you simply need to identify the shape of the room and the shape of each wall. It's that easy. There are only five basic room shapes and four basic wall shapes from which to choose. There are variables to these shapes, but that does not interfere with the simplicity of the Visual Coordinations formula. The variables, including window alcoves or other pockets of space that extend outside the central room area, form a basic shape as well. Once you have identified the shapes, you can then follow the specific Visual Coordinations guidelines for placing furniture to match the particular room. The guidelines will do the thinking for you.

## The Shape of Your Room

Let's start with the five basic room shapes: rectangle, square, oblong, L, and odd-angle. The easiest way to figure out the shape of your room is to look down and follow the lines where the walls and floor meet, skipping over any variables. The shape of the room is determined at floor level, so don't look up. (The lines of the ceiling can throw you off. I will discuss this more fully later.) So, which of the following shapes matches the contours of your room?

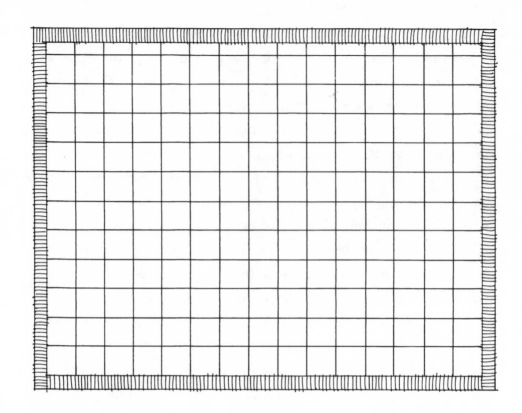

## THE RECTANGULAR ROOM

This is the most common shape for a room. The rectangle can be found in just about any home or apartment and is essential to both classic and contemporary architecture. Quite often the rectangular room has multiple functions. Some of the world's largest rooms were created in this shape and are used to entertain thousands of people. On the other hand, they can accommodate quiet reading, as in a library, or intimate meals, as in a dining room. In apartments or condominiums, the rectangle is popularly used as a combination living-dining room.

## THE SQUARE ROOM

A square room is the next most common shape and has also long been a part of traditional architecture. Usually square rooms are small and serve only one function. Common examples are dens and bedrooms. In many older homes, the living and dining rooms may be small squares. A large square room is a rarity—large is more often the claim of the rectangle. Although the square is common in homes and apartments, it troubles many homeowners because of it space limitations. You'll be happy to learn that the placement formula has sure-fire solutions for making the small square feel larger, more useful, and far more interesting.

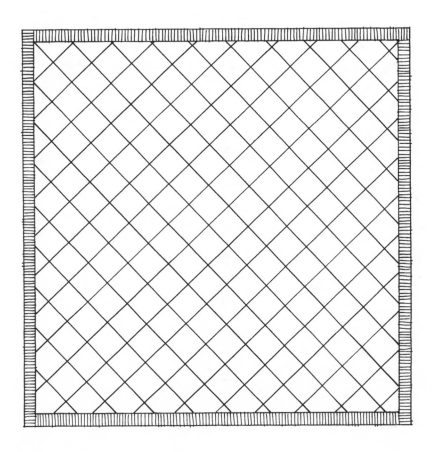

# THE OBLONG ROOM

This room shape—which is long and very narrow—can be likened to a bowling alley. Don't fall into the trap of treating it as a rectangle. The oblong has a distinct set of problems that the rectangle does not

share. Without a doubt, this room shape causes the most grief when it comes to furniture placement. Oblong rooms are frequently found in apartments, condominiums, add-ons, garden rooms, and verandahs. A familiar example is a hallway, a space that is not very conducive to large or numerous pieces of furniture, especially when it serves as a passage. Many people automatically make the mistake of lining furniture up against the two side walls of an oblong room, as they might in a hallway.

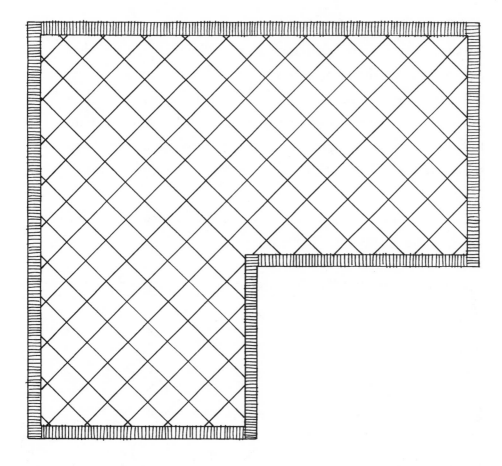

## THE L-SHAPED ROOM

This room shape is formed when two seemingly separate spaces—usually two rectangles—come together to form one. The L is a modern architectural construct, which surfaced in the 1950s with the birth of ranch-style homes. Most often, this multiple-use room functions as a living-dining combination. While it is most common in houses, this shape can also be found in apartments. The problem that many homeowners face with an L-shaped room is making the longer and shorter arms feel as if they are flowing together; instead some people try to decorate the two arms as completely separate areas. Combining them is important, and with the placement technique, it does not need to be confusing or frustrating.

## THE ODD-ANGLE ROOM

Finally we come to the odd-angle room. When reading this shape, it is extremely important that you keep your visual focus down. I stress this because it took me a long time to realize that rooms with architectural interference in the floor lines—a cut-off corner or built-in furniture—can be categorized separately from rectangular or square-shaped rooms. This shape has its own set of rules for furniture placement.

Architectural interference exists wherever a corner is cut off with one or more of the following features:

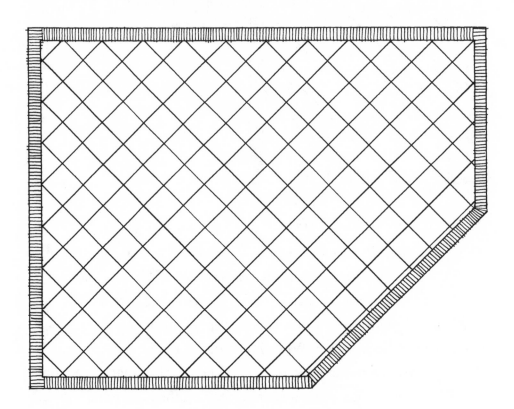

- Cut-off walls running on a 45-degree angle across a corner
- Steps up or down into a room, causing the same 45-degree angle across the floor even if the walls are not affected
- Corner fireplace
- Angled bay window
- Angled counter or pass-through

Certain built-ins can turn a room into an odd-angle. They include built-in bookcases or shelving, entertainment centers that are angled across a corner, corner cabinets, and other movable furniture built specifically to fit a corner.

The illustration shows only one corner cut off, but a room may have more than one cut-off corner and still be considered odd-angle. For example, with a fireplace in one corner and a cabinet in another, the room has two cut-offs.

Odd-angle rooms are more common in newer architecture and are found mainly in space-conscious apartments and condominiums. Even though movable corner cabinets have been around for a long time, they were seldom identified as the makers of odd-angle rooms— until now.

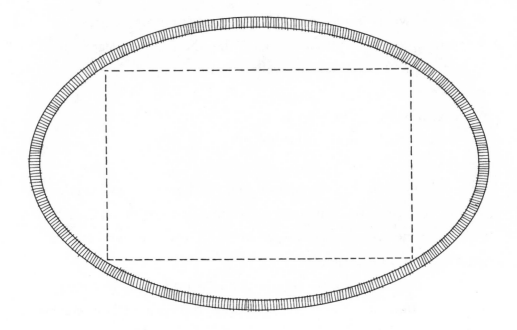

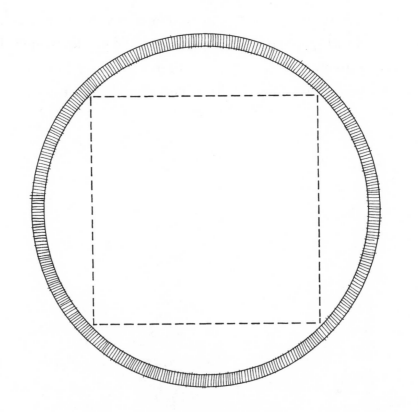

## THE OVAL OR ROUND ROOM

If you're lucky enough to have an oval room, you're either the President of the United States or the mistress of a grand estate. In either case, treat this room as a rectangle (I will explain the reasons later). If you have a round room, chances are your home either dates from the Jeffersonian era or is contemporary. Treat this room as a square, and follow the appropriate furniture placement rules.

Once you've determined the basic shape of your room, you may want to indicate the windows and doorways on these illustrations. Simply mark the approximate area where your architectural features are so you have a visual aid as you continue through the process. Keep in mind, however, that you will be working in the middle of a real-life room as you work, so it's not necessary to use the drawings.

# The Shape of Your Walls

Once you have identified the shape of your room, the next step in reading the architecture is to figure out the shape of the walls. To do this, look in the opposite direction: turn your eyes to where the ceiling and walls come together. Just as the floor line gives shape to the room, the ceiling line gives shape to the wall. Be sure to read each wall shape—one at a time—because most rooms have two or more wall shapes within their space. You'll be working with one shape and one space at a time throughout the entire process, so it's important to understand each step and finish it completely before moving to the next one. Not only will this eliminate frustration; it will also save you time. Identifying your architectural game board is easy when you realize there are a total of just four basic wall shapes to recognize. Choose from the following:

## THE FLAT WALL

Every home has a flat or straight-lined wall somewhere in its midst. It is the leading wall shape in all ages and styles of architecture. Over the years, I've discovered that many homeowners think their walls do not have a shape because they are flat. Let me remind you that flat is a shape, and also an architectural line. You'll find that it is one of the most versatile lines to work with when placing furniture and art, so don't underestimate its value.

Because the dome shape is so uncommon in a home, I don't offer much explanation here, but if you do have one, treat it as a flat wall when placing furniture and art.

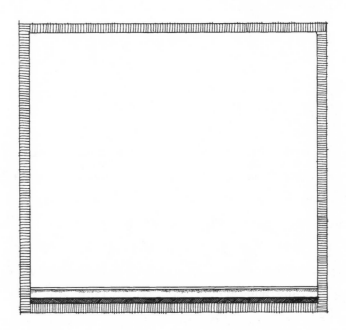

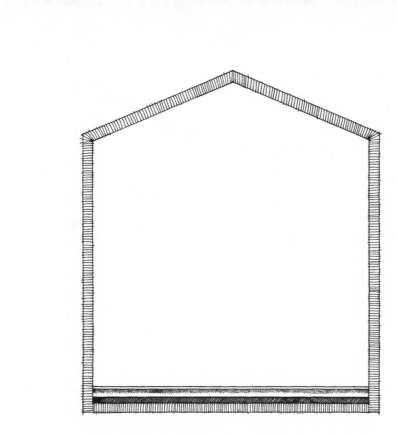

## THE CATHEDRAL WALL

The cathedral wall is more common to houses than apartments and has been an important part of architecture through the ages. As the name implies, this wall shape conjures up thoughts of church. We are reminded of a long sanctuary, with enormous ceilings rising high in the middle.

With a cathedral wall, your room will probably also have two different wall shapes. Usually the two end walls are cathedral while the two side walls are flat. The basic cathedral wall makes a dramatic statement in any room and is inspiring to work with when placing furniture and art. Much less common in household architecture are four cathedral walls that come together in the center of a room to form a pyramid shape. Although this contour is not considered basic to our formula, you should still read one wall shape at a time.

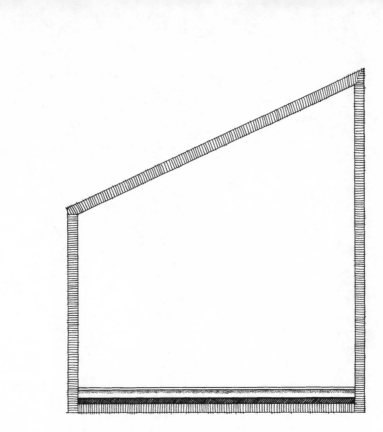

## THE PITCHED WALL

To envision this shape, just think of a chicken coop. The form certainly has more upscale uses, especially in contemporary architecture, and can be found more often in homes than in apartments or condominiums. The pitched wall is fun to work with, and as with its sister, the cathedral, most rooms with this shape will have two pitched walls and two flat walls, one higher than the other.

## THE STEP-UP WALL

With this name, stairs come immediately to mind. The horizontal and vertical lines of a step-up wall often go unnoticed when placing furniture or art, but they can become a problem if not understood properly. The step-up is common in older homes, add-ons, landings, and lofts. Don't mistake the step-up for a ledge; the shape of this wall comes from its flat overall surface.

You have now completed reading the architecture of your room. I hope you're starting to look at your home in a new way and are discovering how much the architecture impacts the style of the rooms, and eventually the placement of the furniture. If you have a floor or wall shape that does not exactly match one of the selections described here, try to work the puzzle. Maybe by combining two of the shapes, you can construct a close match to your room. Otherwise, follow the guidelines for the shape that most closely matches one of the basic forms.

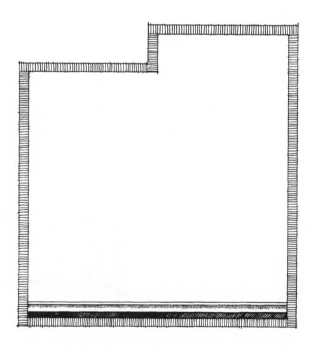

# 4

# Placing the Furniture

Now that the roots of your tree have been established, it's time to start moving up to the trunk. Before you begin this step and start bringing your belongings out of the holding area, take a moment to clear your mind. Disregard all the decorating myths and notions you've been absorbing over the past years. Forget the old image of the room. Now put yourself in the room you're about to rearrange, keeping your mind clear and ready to work with a new way of looking at decorating.

# The Warm-Up

In Visual Coordinations, we think of furniture in broad terms. Not only do I include the basics, such as tables, chairs, sofas, and cabinets, but I also consider rugs, lamps, potted trees, and large plants to be furniture. When you rearrange your furniture, the first item you place in the living space is the largest seating piece—in most cases, the sofa. It should address or look into the architectural focal point you have selected; in other words, place it directly opposite the focal point. You can vary the distance between the piece and the focal point as you continue through the Visual Coordinations process and as you bring more items into the room. For now, just place it at a comfortable distance.

This one move automatically connects the contents of your room to the architecture. I have been in thousands of homes where the single biggest mistake is that the sofa has been placed in front of a large window or fireplace, looking away from the focal point. Don't make this mistake, or the system will not succeed.

The focal point sets the position point for the largest seating piece; all other furniture, including pianos, lamps, large plants, potted trees, and area rugs, then falls into place according to it and to the architectural lines of the room. Please read through the Furniture Placement Tips, below, before you start to move any more furniture into the room. And before you bring anything out of the holding area, let's review some of the ideas you want to keep in the back of your mind as you proceed.

As you place your furniture within the room, you want to follow the tacking principle. Like a sailboat that tacks in a zigzag direction to maneuver forward, you should place your items as if they existed on a grid, situating one piece in relation to the next. (In the illustrations, the direction of the grid is represented by dashed lines.)

In my experience, I have found that angling furniture works quite effectively, especially in square and L-shaped rooms. It creates a pocket of space behind the pieces, giving you more room to layer in another piece. The room actually feels bigger with more furniture in it, and angling forces you to use all of the space instead of lining up everything against the walls. Angling furniture also allows for more fluidity and movement within the room, from both an aesthetic standpoint and a practical one, as you walk through the space.

Keep in mind the checkpoints that we discussed in Chapter 1: creating weaving traffic patterns and peaks and valleys. As you may recall, a weaving traffic pattern means that the furniture placement allows for a clear passage through the room without it being a straight path from one doorway to the next. It forces one to maneuver around large pieces or groupings of smaller furniture. Regarding peaks and valleys, think of them as volume and pause when you're placing the furniture. Volume exists wherever you create a grouping of furniture. Pause is the empty space or area between furniture groupings. Both are equally important; volume cannot exist without pause, nor can pause happen without volume. Being aware of this checkpoint means that you should not fill every nook and cranny, especially an empty area around a large grouping. Allowing the pause to call attention to the volume is much more effective than cluttering the area.

As you begin to group furniture throughout your room, weight automatically enters the space. This serves as the base for balancing the height elements that you will add later. The illustration below shows how tacking works with both placement and weight.

Don't worry about having either too much or too little furniture; the solution lies in expanding and contracting. This is exactly what it sounds like: If you have a sparsely furnished room, you should exploit as much of your room's space as you can—expand your furniture pattern. To create the illusion of space in a crowded room, you need to

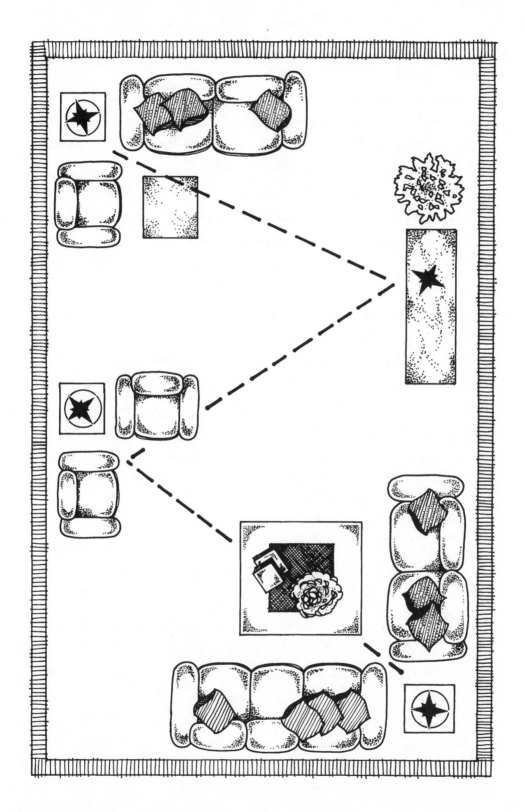

contract or tighten the furniture pattern by clustering or layering items.

Don't be afraid to use items from other rooms. I was in a home once in which most of the furniture in the living room really belonged in the den, and the den furniture was better suited to the living room. I have seen this pattern hundreds of times in my rearranging career, and it's smart to keep it in mind: The fact that a piece of furniture has always been in a certain place doesn't mean it looks best there. In fact, if you're taking the trouble to rearrange your belongings, chances are that some of your furniture would benefit from a new position in your home.

My last reminder is to start looking at your furniture pieces as individual three-dimensional shapes instead of as functional objects. For example, a sofa can be a long, horizontal rectangle, a high-backed chair can be a vertical oval on top of a square, and a coffee table can be a low circle or rectangle. Remembering the image of a puzzle, with pieces of various shapes and sizes, conditions your mind to view your furniture in this way; it will help you to eventually create the complete picture.

## Furniture Placement Tips

❖ The natural order of placing your furniture is to start with the largest pieces of seating furniture and work your way down to the smaller items, one piece at a time. After you place all of the seating, fill the pockets with the remaining pieces, again starting with the larger and working to the smaller.

❖ Regardless of the size of your room or the amount of furniture you have, bring your items out into the room instead of lining them up along the walls. After all, you live *in* your room, not around it.

Note that this does not affect the rules of contracting or expanding.

❖ Don't separate like or matching sofas. Corner them together. Never place two sofas or love seats facing each other. This sets up a separation of weight that cannot be counterbalanced, and it upsets the tacking principle.

❖ Keep like chairs together. Chairs of the same size, shape, or color must stay together. Separating these pairs or sets dilutes their impact and gives the room a scattered look. (Spreading similar items around the room should not be confused with expanding the furniture.)

❖ Sectional sofas are an exception to the rule about keeping sets together. Like wall units, they can overpower a room, making one area too heavy in weight. Pulling one or two pieces from the sectional to form another point of furniture weight gives the counterbalance that is needed. Plus, your sectional then serves more purposes.

❖ If you have three or more pieces in a movable wall unit, consider removing one section and placing it diagonally across the room in one of the pause or pocket areas. This will counterbalance the weight and height of the wall unit set. If you have too much furniture weight on one side of your room, it will appear to be toppling over like a sinking ship.

❖ Avoid the temptation to stuff potted trees into empty corners. This will not exploit their natural beauty. In other words, make them a part of your furnishings.

❖ Area rugs are meant to serve as anchors. Use them to secure a furniture grouping, to connect and extend a piece of furniture, or to identify an architectural space such as a foyer or hallway. Do not place them randomly.

❖ The television is never an architectural focal point unless it is

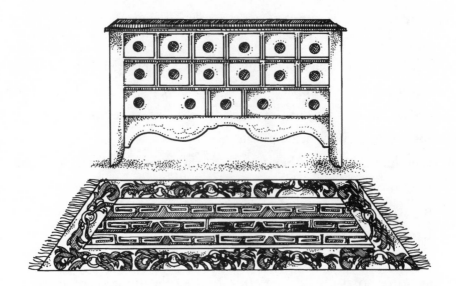

housed in a built-in wall unit that has been selected as the focal point of the room. After all, televisions and cable outlets are movable. Always place the television *after* you've completed the seating furniture.

❖ Furniture weight combinations that can be placed together to form right angles (or corners) include sofa-sofa, sofa-chair, love seat–love seat, love seat–chair, and chair-chair.

## Pockets of Space

Once you've placed the seating furniture and established the guidelines for your living space, the stage is set for additional pocket or side pieces. The space that is left provides you with a template or guide for what goes where, as you match the size and shape of each remaining piece to the space available. As we walk through our rooms, we'll pop in more furniture to give you a clear idea of some of the many pocket possibilities.

# Furniture Placement Techniques

In Chapter 3, "Reading the Architecture," you identified the room and wall shapes you'll be working with. Now you can learn the basic techniques for placing furniture in your particular room. Although the ten-step guidelines, below, appear to be the same for each room shape, if you pay close attention you'll notice slight—but important—variations. I have deliberately repeated the guidelines for each room shape to make it easy for you to follow. You'll find it a handy reference to use as you work in your room.

I've also included additional information geared to each specific room and wall shape, providing you with some alternatives that may suit your specific needs. In the illustrations, the room shapes are all drawn from above, as aerial views, so that you can see the furniture placement in relation to the floor. The wall shapes are illustrated from a straight-ahead, eye-level vantage point, so that you can see how the furniture aligns with the connection points of the ceiling and wall. The illustrations are meant to serve as examples only, since the location of the architectural focal point and the placement of the furniture will vary.

I've also included illustrations and suggestions for creating what I call "pocket possibilities" for the various room and wall shapes. These are my suggestions, based on the shape of the room and the furnishings. They are not meant to match exactly with the items that you have but will give you some ideas as to how you can rearrange your own things. Pocket possibilities are simply examples that give new meaning—and new uses—to all that furniture you never quite knew how to use effectively. Those of you with minimal furniture, don't fret. Place what you do have according to the guidelines, and then shop at your convenience—budget and taste in tow—for the furniture you now know will work in your home. Not knowing what to look for keeps many of us from looking at all. Now you can shop for just the right piece, knowing that it is guaranteed to work.

## THE RECTANGULAR ROOM

WHAT TO DO

1. Place the sofa (or largest seating piece) across from the architectural focal point, looking into it. Attach additional piece or pieces in an L pattern as shown.

2. Refer to the dotted guidelines. Place a seating or seat grouping diagonally across from first grouping.

3. Continue to tack seating furniture across from your starting point (the sofa).

4. Once all seating furniture has been positioned according to the basic guidelines of tacking the weight, fill in the empty pockets of space with the remaining large pieces of furniture, based on the size and shape of both the space and the piece.

5. Expand or contract furniture placement.

6. Connect or layer smaller pieces of furniture, such as end tables, occasional tables, and ottomans, to the new pattern.

7. Place area rugs to anchor furniture groupings, extend furniture pieces, and enhance hallways and foyers.

8. Place large trees and plants so that they connect to the new furniture pattern—avoiding those corners!

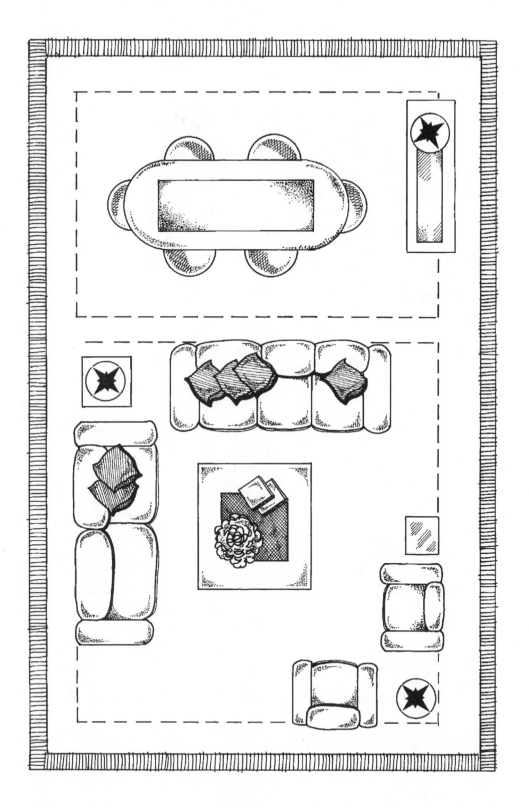

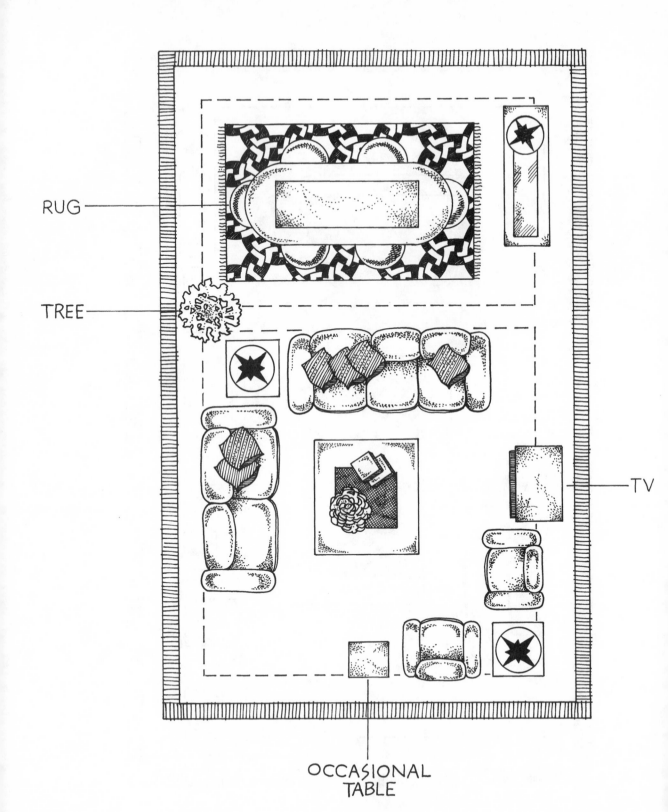

RUG

TREE

TV

OCCASIONAL
TABLE

66

9. Place lighting to anchor each furniture grouping.

10. Review the checkpoints. Is there a weaving traffic pattern? Does lighting automatically create a diagonal or triangular pattern? If so, you've completed this step correctly. From this point on, you will simply be connecting or layering all art and accessories to the furniture you have just placed.

MORE BASICS

The rectangular room is often used to house two distinct living areas, such as living-dining, living-entry, living-reading, or living-entertaining. For an extra large rectangular room, the multi-use possibilities are endless. The living–dining room combo is the most common multi-use for a rectangular room, so that is what I have illustrated. Don't feel limited to this setup, however. You can work with the formula to suit any situation you would like. For instance, if you have a separate room for dining, consider using the allocated space as a reading, game, or television area. This offers you the advantage of having two distinct sections in the same room, while it is really still just a living room. Whatever use you choose for your rectangular room, continue to set your furniture weight diagonally across from the sofa and love seat, as shown, to counterbalance each other; or tack the weight throughout the room.

POCKET POSSIBILITY

One of the most common and important additions to a room is the television. You may need to expand the position of the chairs, but remember, nothing is nailed to the floor, so you can make adjustments. Don't be afraid to experiment with expanding and contracting in your placement project. You may also need to expand the sofa and love seat

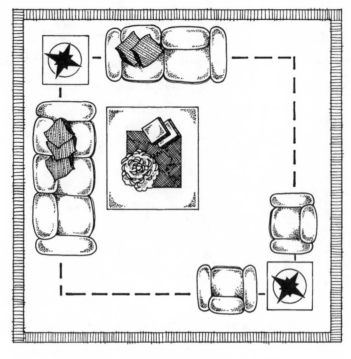

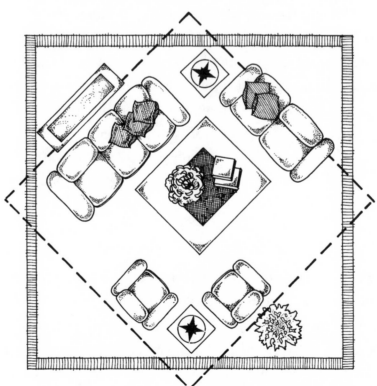

a bit. Now we add a small occasional table next to one chair. This can also be a bushy plant or a magazine rack. Placing a tree near the connecting sofa and lamp serves both as added height and as a gentle room divider between the living and dining areas. An area rug anchoring the dining table brings a defining touch of color and weight.

## THE SQUARE ROOM

I have supplied two illustrations to offer you a choice of guidelines. As I mentioned, angling furniture in a square room is a great way to uncover more space and adds to the room's overall energy and spirit.

### WHAT TO DO

1. Place the sofa (or largest seating piece) across from the architectural focal point, looking into it. Attach additional piece or pieces in an L pattern as shown.

2. Refer to the dotted guidelines.

3. Continue to tack seating furniture across from your starting point (the sofa).

4. Once all seating furniture has been positioned according to the basic guidelines of tacking the weight, fill in the empty pockets of space with the remaining large pieces of furniture, based on the size and shape of both the space and the piece.

5. Expand or contract furniture placement.

6. Connect or layer smaller pieces of furniture, such as end tables, occasional tables, and ottomans, to the new pattern.

7. Use area rugs to anchor furniture groupings, extend furniture pieces, and enhance hallways and foyers.

8. Place large trees and plants so that they connect to the new furniture pattern—avoiding those corners!

9. Place lighting to anchor each furniture grouping.

10. Review the checkpoints. Is there a weaving traffic pattern? Does lighting automatically create a diagonal or triangular pattern? If so, you've completed this step correctly. From this point on, you will simply be connecting or layering all art and accessories to the furniture you have just placed.

### MORE BASICS

Square rooms are usually smaller than other shapes and qualify as single-use rooms, such as dens, libraries, or offices. Even if you do not have a square room in your house, you can apply the techniques to many of the other forms, especially rectangles and L-shaped rooms.

### POCKET POSSIBILITY

Setting up this room according to the first illustration (in which the furniture placement is squared) limits the pocket possibilities. If you use the second option (in which the furniture is angled), the possibilities are dramatically extended.

However, if you're not yet brave enough to try angling, not to worry. You can still add some pieces to the pockets of space that are available. As you can see, we've managed to fit in a television, occasional table, and ottoman quite comfortably. Popping in a tree between the television and the reading chair adds the height and weight needed to counterbalance the weight of the sofa and love seat.

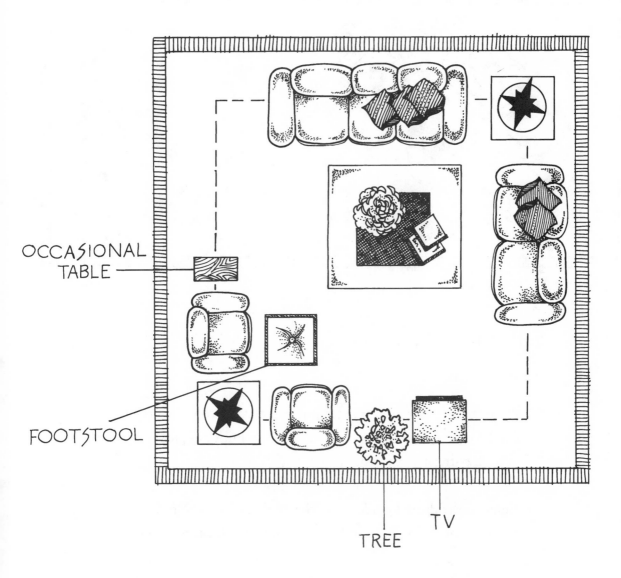

OCCASIONAL TABLE

FOOTSTOOL

TREE

TV

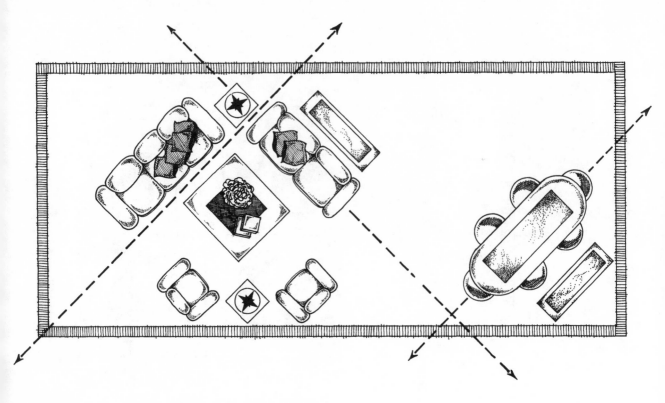

## THE OBLONG ROOM

WHAT TO DO

1. Place the sofa (or largest seating piece) across from the architectural focal point, looking into it. Attach additional piece or pieces in an L pattern as shown.

2. Refer to the dotted guidelines. The angle allows you to use the space in the room without blocking movement through the room.

3. Continue to tack seating furniture across from your starting point (the sofa).

4. Once all seating furniture has been positioned according to the basic guidelines of tacking the weight, fill in the empty pockets of

space with the remaining large pieces of furniture, based on the size and shape of both the space and the piece.

5. Expand or contract furniture placement.

6. Connect or layer smaller pieces of furniture, such as end tables, occasional tables, and ottomans, to the new pattern.

7. Use area rugs to anchor furniture groupings, extend furniture pieces, and enhance hallways and foyers.

8. Place large trees and plants so that they connect to the new furniture pattern—avoiding those corners!

9. Place lighting to anchor each furniture grouping.

10. Review the checkpoints. Is there a weaving traffic pattern? Does lighting automatically create a diagonal or triangular pattern? If so, you have completed this step correctly. From this point on, you'll simply be connecting or layering all art and accessories to the furniture you've just placed.

MORE BASICS

Oblong, or "bowling alley," rooms are the most neglected shapes in terms of placing furniture. Many people don't understand how to work with the space and end up lining furniture against the two side walls in the mistaken belief that this will make the room look larger. Let me emphasize again that using all of the space in a room makes it look and feel larger. Placing furniture along the walls only creates a longer bowling alley.

By following the guidelines and gently pulling the furniture into

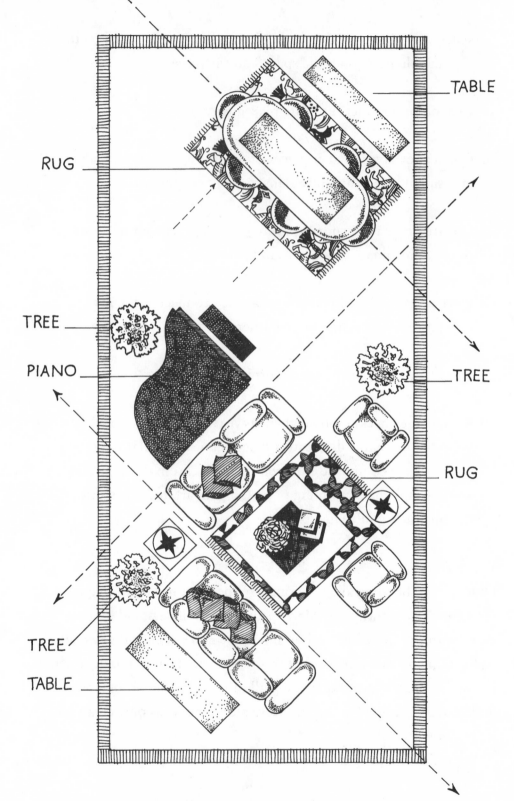

TABLE

RUG

TREE

PIANO

TREE

RUG

TREE

TABLE

the room on an angle, you're forced to weave through the room instead of "bowl" down it. Best of all, the pockets of space behind the angled furniture give you ideal areas in which to layer pieces. The room can actually accommodate more furniture.

### POCKET POSSIBILITY

The first thing we did in the oblong room is move the table behind the love seat, connecting it to the sofa. With a new pocket of space between the love seat and the dining area, there is now enough room for a grand piano. Next, we further define the living and dining areas by adding area rugs, keeping them angled like the furniture. You may need to extend the dining table out into the room a little for the rug to anchor it evenly. Adding three trees gives the feeling of a leisurely walk in the park, instead of a swift roll down the bowling lane. By contracting the two chairs, there is enough space in the corner for a television or even a desk, provided it is angled, of course.

## THE L-SHAPED ROOM

I have included two illustrations with different sets of guidelines; the first one represents the average-size L, and the other is an oversize L-shaped room.

For the former, follow the "What to Do" steps, working one section of space at a time. For the oversize L-shaped room, you must establish three separate areas (even if the room is used for one purpose), all set in a square pattern. Furniture in the two arms of the L should be arranged on a square grid pattern, while the elbow space of the L is set on an angle. This angle provides the subtle connection among the three separate areas of use. When working with this space, be sure to rearrange one section at a time.

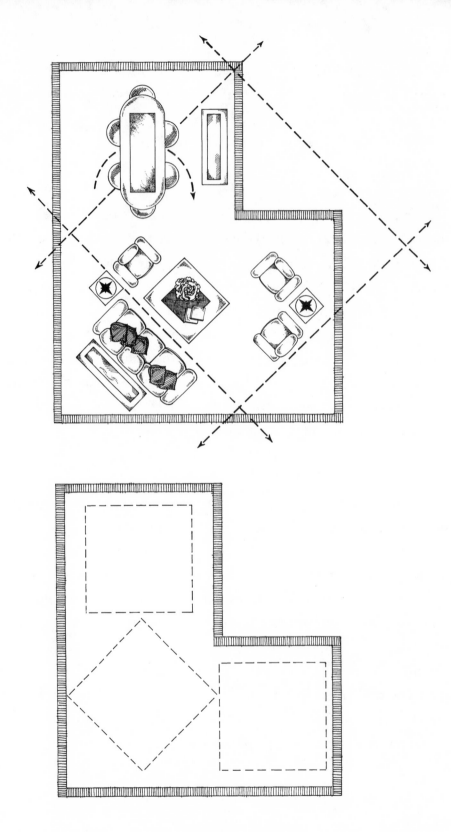

1. Place the sofa (or largest seating piece) across from the architectural focal point, looking into it. Attach the additional piece or pieces in an L pattern as shown.

2. Refer to the dotted guidelines. Angle the dining table whenever possible.

3. Continue to tack seating furniture across from your starting point (the sofa).

4. Once all seating furniture has been positioned according to the basic guidelines of tacking the weight, fill in the empty pockets of space with the remaining large pieces of furniture, based on the size and shape of both the space and the piece.

5. Expand or contract furniture placement.

6. Connect or layer smaller pieces of furniture, such as end tables, occasional tables, and ottomans, to the new pattern.

7. Use area rugs to anchor furniture groupings, extend furniture pieces, and enhance hallways and foyers.

8. Place large trees and plants so that they connect to the new furniture pattern—avoiding those corners!

9. Place lighting to anchor each furniture grouping.

10. Review the checkpoints. Is there a weaving traffic pattern? Does lighting automatically create a diagonal or triangular pattern? If so, you have completed this step correctly. From this point on, you'll simply be connecting or layering all art and accessories to the furniture you've just placed.

## MORE BASICS

Like the rectangular space, the L-shaped room usually serves many purposes, often as a dining–living–family room combination. The biggest problem with arranging furniture in a room of this shape is getting the entire space to flow together without an abrupt stop from one area to another. Angling the furniture creates a beautiful feeling of unity, making the space divisions more subtle. There is no reason why the table has to be parallel with the walls, and angling helps the flow from the dining area to the living room.

## POCKET POSSIBILITY

By moving the side piece in the dining room to the other side and placing it on an angle, we are able to shift the dining table to the same angle. The television is an effective way to soften the corner wall. The generous pocket of space behind the two chairs becomes a welcome home to two bookcases or display cabinets. Popping a tree in between the sofa and chair—and a shorter tree next to the television—completes a room that is now comfortably full of furniture but not crowded. The addition of an area rug under the dining table balances the weight between the living and dining areas. It also gives you an excuse to invite your friends over for that long-promised dinner party.

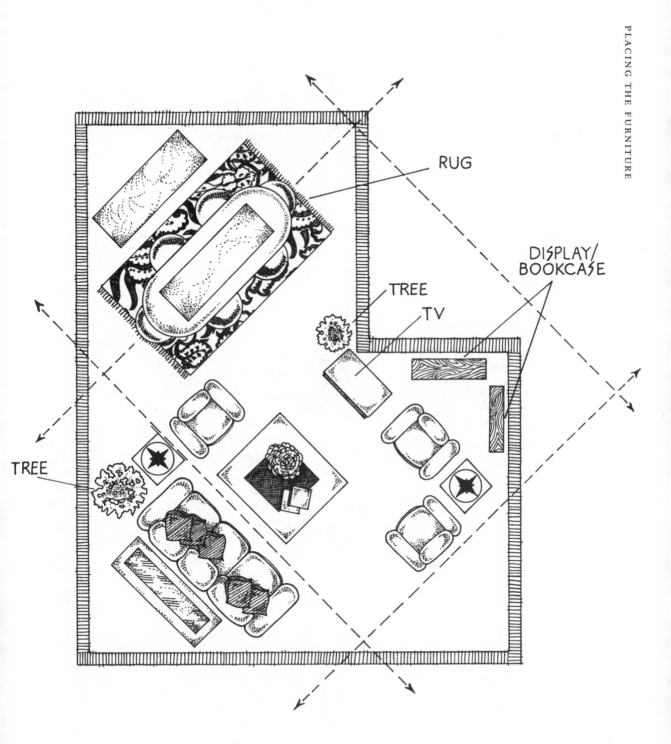

RUG

DISPLAY/
BOOKCASE

TREE

TV

TREE

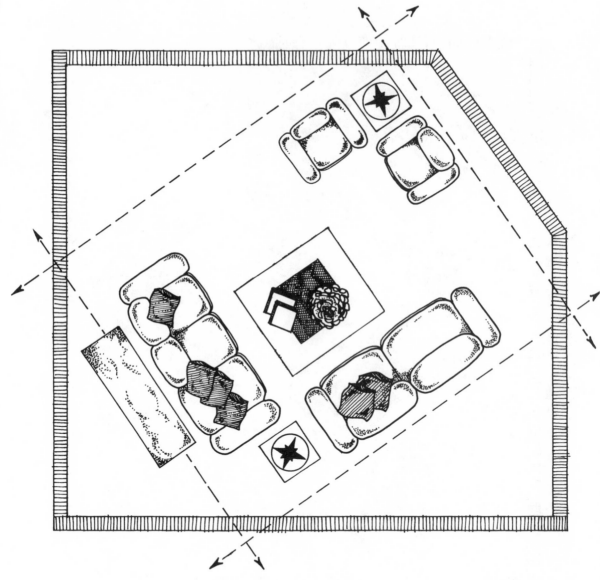

# THE ODD-ANGLE ROOM

WHAT TO DO

1. Place the sofa (or largest seating piece) across from the architectural focal point, looking into it. Attach additional piece or pieces in an L pattern as shown.

2. Refer to the dotted guidelines. No matter how small the angle of the architecture, you must place all furniture in relation to the angled guidelines.

3. Continue to tack seating furniture across from your starting point (the sofa).

4. Once all seating furniture has been positioned according to the basic guidelines of tacking the weight, fill in the empty pockets of space with the remaining large pieces of furniture, based on the size and shape of both the space and the piece.

5. Expand or contract furniture placement.

6. Connect or layer smaller pieces of furniture, such as end tables, occasional tables, and ottomans, to the new pattern.

7. Use area rugs to anchor furniture groupings, extend furniture pieces, and enhance hallways and foyers.

8. Place large trees and plants so that they connect to the new furniture pattern—avoiding those corners!

9. Place lighting to anchor each furniture grouping.

10. Review the checkpoints. Is there a weaving traffic pattern? Does lighting automatically create a diagonal or triangular pattern? If so, you have completed this step correctly. From this point on, you'll simply be connecting or layering all art and accessories to the furniture you've just placed.

## MORE BASICS

Odd-angle rooms are becoming more prevalent with modern architecture; if you have a fairly new home, you'll probably be working within these guidelines. Regardless of the room's purpose, remember to work with, not against, the odd architectural angle. Set your furniture on an angle that duplicates the architectural one.

## POCKET POSSIBILITY

Go with the architectural angle to open up the odd-angled room to a wealth of pocket possibilities. Expand those chairs and add a television. How about a bookcase or display cabinet behind the love seat? Two trees counterbalance the height and weight beautifully. The occasional table is ideal for the reader in the family. Anchor the entire setting with a colorful area rug placed on the angle, and voilà! You have solved the placement puzzle of that old nemesis, the odd-angled room.

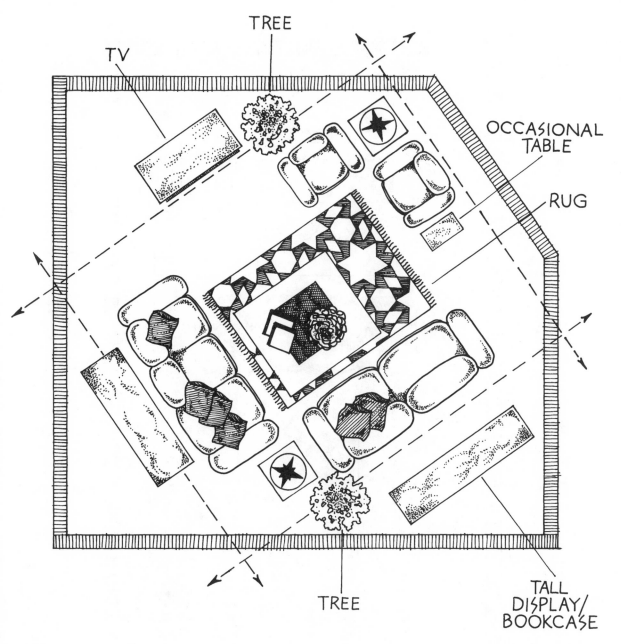

TREE

TV

OCCASIONAL TABLE

RUG

TREE

TALL DISPLAY/ BOOKCASE

# OVAL ROOM

Follow the guidelines for a rectangular room.

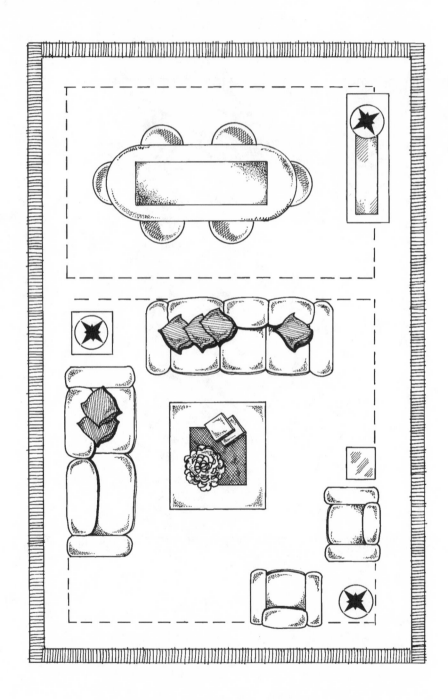

# ROUND ROOM

Follow the guidelines for a square room.

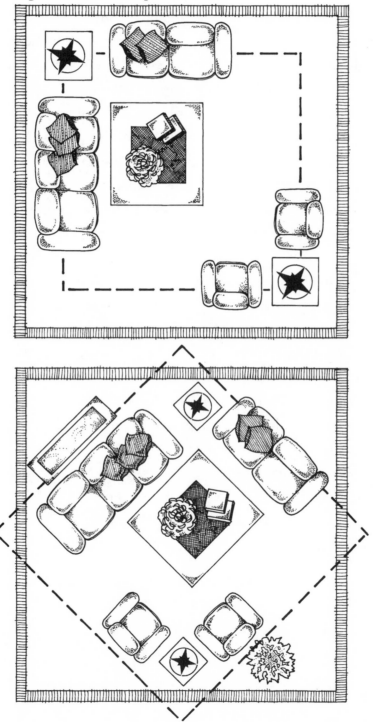

# Working with Wall Shapes

Defining the shape of the walls surrounding your room is another important step in furniture placement. In Chapter 3 you identified the shapes you'll be working with. Now we'll review Visual Coordinations guidelines for placing furniture in relation to each wall type.

The guidelines for wall shapes are fixed and cannot be compromised, with one exception—the flat wall. This is the only shape where you can build furniture weight and height at any given point.

In placing furniture according to wall shapes, think tall-to-tall and short-to-short. As the ceiling rises, so should the height of the furniture. The low point of the ceiling should contain the lower, or shorter, pieces.

If you don't have tall furniture, don't worry. You'll be able to add height to your pieces with art. (More about that in the next chapter.) Furniture weight is the base for building height where you need it.

Remember that when you are placing furniture, you can create a pattern of peaks and valleys within your room. Think of your furniture weight as the base of a mountain. As you layer other pieces of furniture and art to the new arrangement, peaks will start to build. Every mountain has a base of weight from which it forms height, rising to a peak. The spaces between the peaks will form the valleys, echoing the beauty and fluid motion found in nature.

Once again, the illustrations are meant to serve as examples only, since your selection of furniture will vary.

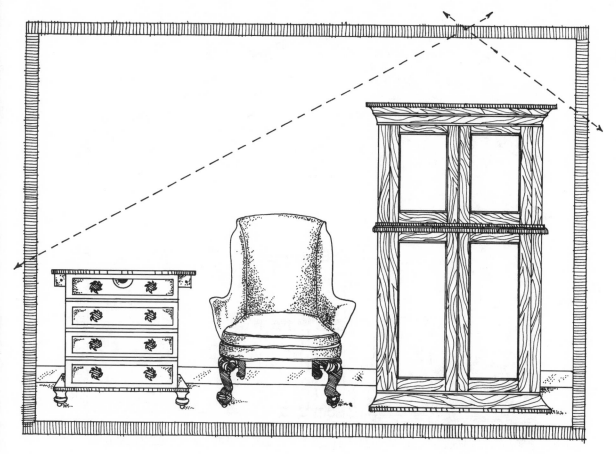

## THE FLAT WALL

With the flat wall, you have the freedom to build a peak wherever you wish. There is nothing in the architecture telling you to do otherwise. The illustration shows the peak to the right side of the wall, but the guidelines work just as well if you choose to form a peak in the center or to the left; it doesn't matter where the peak is, as long as you create one.

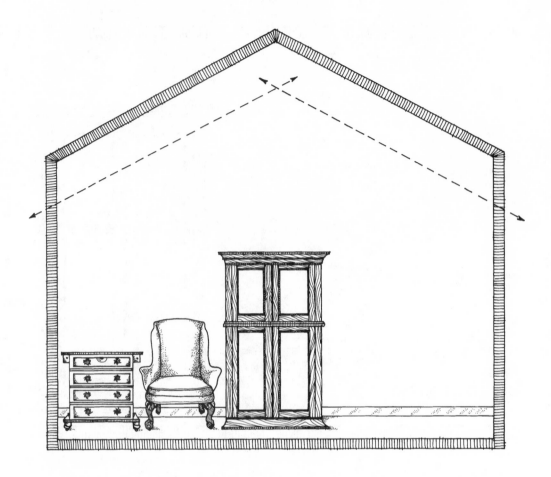

## THE CATHEDRAL WALL

As the ceiling rises, so should your furniture—the tall-to-tall rule. Your tallest furniture can be a little to the left or right of center as long as it is close enough to feel connected to the high point of the wall. If it's placed too far away from the center, you'll lose the effect.

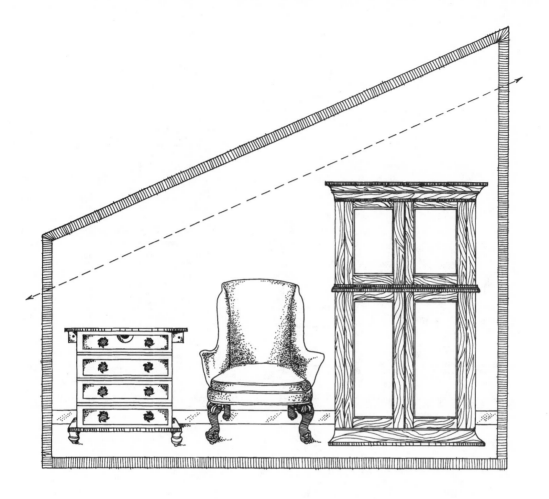

## THE PITCHED WALL

Simply follow the lines of the architecture; the ceiling line offers the perfect guide for placing tall or heavy pieces of furniture. Tall-to-tall, short-to-short never fails. If you don't have furniture that is tall enough to balance the height of the wall, remember that you can extend and add height using art and accessories.

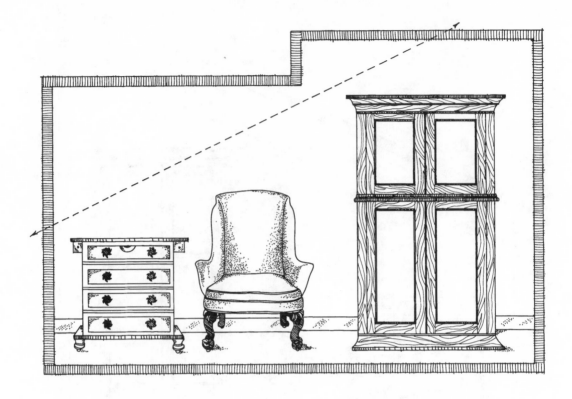

## THE STEP-UP WALL

The ceiling line leaves only one choice for height on this shape wall. Avoid shoving a piece of furniture into the lower section of the wall just because it looks as if it will fit. It is much better to give it space to breathe on the highest section of the wall. Our tall-to-tall rule leaves you with no other choices.

# 5

# Hanging the Art

Are you the kind of person who moves into a house
and hangs art on the nails left by the former resident?
Or does your art sit on the floor for weeks because you're

afraid to put holes in
the plaster until you're
absolutely sure where
you want to hang it?
Do you always end up
hanging art too high
because it looked good
to your husband when
he was standing in
front of it?

It seems as if hanging art should be an easy task—bang a nail in the wall and voilà—but for anyone who has spent frustrating hours getting a framed portrait or a mirror to look just right, you know how much of a nuisance hanging art can be. It doesn't have to be so difficult, though. Visual Coordinations teaches you the key to solving the problem: knowing exactly where to hang art.

## The Warm-Up

While it is difficult to define "art"—some consider it only significant signed works, worthy of high insurance premiums—to me it is a very personal reflection of your background, travel experiences, and aesthetic taste. Therefore, in following this technique, please think of "art" as anything that you choose to hang on your walls. (Sculptures and table-top art are considered accessories, and we'll discuss them later.)

While we all know that art adds color and personality to a room, making the room's style distinctive and clearly your own, it can do even more. Art should not just hang on a wall, unrelated to anything but itself. That kind of display is appropriate in museums, but not in homes. Art should be connected to and integrated with everything else in your home. And it should be used to highlight and beautify the other pieces of furniture or accessories. Artworks are especially handy if you need to amplify and extend a piece of furniture or an architectural space in order to create a stronger presence.

Once you have your furniture in place, you're ready to tackle the art. You'll want to keep your tools nearby, especially a hammer, nails, a pencil, a tape measure, and some spackling compound. Remember that it's all right to make a mistake—that's what spackle is for. Don't feel overwhelmed when you read through the tips below. Just take it one picture at a time.

# Frames

The first step in thinking about art as more than just a pretty picture is to focus on the frame. You've probably never looked closely at the shape of your pictures, but this is an important part of deciding how to properly align a piece with the room's structure. As you learned in the chapter on furniture, there are a limited number of basic shapes that you should be able to recognize and match up with your belongings. When dealing with art, there are really only six basic frame shapes, but they come in hundreds of different sizes.

You're probably very familiar with your pieces, but scan the art you wish to hang in a particular room. Remember that you're not limited to the material in the holding area—you can draw from or give to other rooms if necessary. As you look through the pictures, start to group them according to their basic shapes (be very careful when handling delicate artwork). You may have a little pile of rectangles, a couple of ovals, and one square. Now match those same basic shapes to the contours of your furniture or to an empty space on the wall. For instance, a mantelpiece would match with the horizontal rectangular shape, a low potted plant could match with an oval or circle, and a chair might match with a square frame.

Remember the idea of the puzzle: Your goal is to fit your pieces—in this case the art—into the structure of your room, based on the Visual Coordinations guidelines. Think about size, shape, and color as you're matching the frames and their contents with your furniture and with the architectural lines of the room.

# Tips for Hanging Art

❖ Grouping like shapes (frame-frame or frame-furniture) is the priority.

❖ To enhance wall space, match the shape of the frame to the shape of the wall. For example, don't hang a vertical frame on a horizontal wall.

❖ Don't hang art too high. We spend most of our time in a room sitting, not standing, so it's not appropriate to place a painting at standing eye-level height. Don't place art too far away from the furniture. Keep it attached to the piece of furniture, instead of floating away from it—no more than six inches distance is my rule of thumb.

❖ When hanging a gallery or grouping of art together, lay it out on the floor first to decide the overall size and shape of the arrangement. This prevents mistakes on the wall.

❖ Always hang mirrors across from windows to reflect the natural light or the view. Other functional places for mirrors include foyers and attached to such furniture as dressers and vanities.

❖ Keep pairs and sets of art together. Don't spread them around the room or house.

❖ Keep like colors, finishes, and themes together. Take advantage of any opportunities to match colors of art to upholstery fabric, to connect wood finishes, or to cluster themes of art and furniture together. But the priority is always to match shapes first.

❖ Use art to add height or width where you need it.

❖ It's easier for two people to hang art (providing they agree with one another) than to do it by yourself.

❖ If you make a mistake, don't worry about putting another hole in the wall. Filling in holes is the purpose of the spackling compound.

❖ The best time to spackle is when everything has been removed from the walls.

# HANGING ART

Here is a time-saving method for hanging art at exactly the level you want.

1. SELECT POSITION & HOLD PICTURE UP TO WALL. MAKE A SMALL PENCIL DOT AT FRAME'S EDGE, IN THE CENTER

2. REMOVE ART, LEAVING SMALL DOT

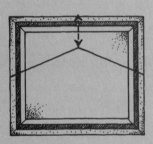

3. MEASURE SPACE FROM FRAME'S EDGE TO CENTER OF TAUT WIRE

4. MEASURE SAME SPACE FROM DOT DOWN—MARK

SET PICTURE HOOK OVER

HANG PICTURE!

- ❖ If the wire on a frame is worn, replace it before you move the art. The move itself could cause a frayed wire to snap, sending the piece crashing to the floor.
- ❖ If you need to buy art for a certain space on the wall, use construction paper, matte board, or even sheets of newspaper cut to the size and shape that suits the space. Gently pin or tack it to the wall to determine the exact size and shape you need.

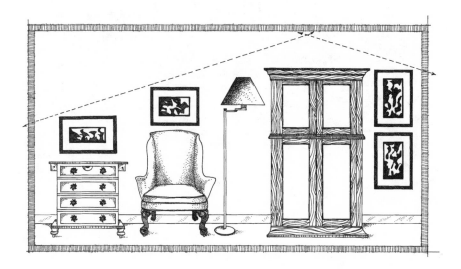

# Gallery of Visual Coordinations Guidelines

### EXTEND FURNITURE AND ENHANCE PEAKS AND VALLEYS.

1. Connect art to furniture, extending pieces up or out.

2. Keep art within peaks and valleys guidelines.

3. Notice the layering or connecting to furniture.

**EXTEND THE SHAPE OF A SOFA OR LOVE SEAT.**

1.  Always look at the shape of your art or grouping, and match the overall shape to the sofa or love seat.

2.  Never hang a single vertical frame above the horizontal shape of a sofa. Pairs or sets of art that form a horizontal shape will work.

3.  Don't hang art too high, or too far away from the furniture. It will seem disconnected from the room's unity.

4.  Don't allow frames to extend beyond the outside edges of furniture.

5. There are numerous frame combinations you can use, provided the overall shape of the furniture is followed.

6. If you're lucky enough to have the same colors in both art and fabric, you'll create beautiful pockets of color that achieve that quality of oneness so integral to a beautiful home.

By following these guidelines, your furniture and art will give the impression of a master plan at work.

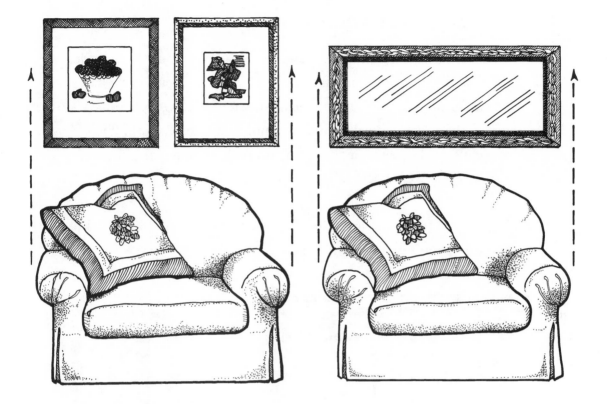

**EXTEND THE SHAPE OF CHAIRS.**

The guidelines for a sofa and love seat also apply to chairs. Again, combinations of art can be used, but on a smaller scale. Matching the color of the art to the fabric of the chair is an added bonus. Make sure the lines of the art extend the lines of the chair.

EXTEND FURNITURE WIDTH AS WELL AS HEIGHT.

1. Connect art to a tall piece of furniture by running it down the side, creating the illusion of making the piece wider. As long as the lines of the furniture are followed, height is not an issue. All that matters in the Visual Coordinations formula is the connection. Pitch those old prohibitions against hanging art low on a wall. Just ask yourself, "Is it connected?"

2. With wood furniture, if the finish of the frame matches that of the furniture, you've created an even more striking tableau.

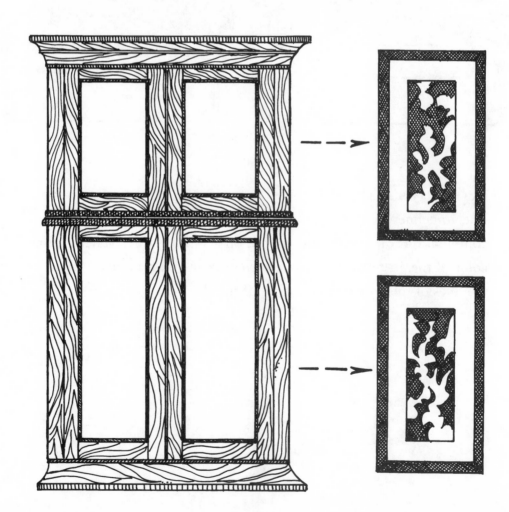

FRAME OUT A PIECE OF FURNITURE.

When you think of framing out, you don't usually think of furniture. Yet in this illustration, you can clearly see that the piece looks taller and wider when art extends its original size and shape.

1. This is the quickest and most exciting way to create a feeling of more weight.

2. The secret to attaching art across the top and down the side of furniture is to make sure that the distance from the piece and the connecting edge of the frame is the same along both the top and the side. This is what makes the two feel like one.

3. A similar finish on furniture and frames adds to the visual impact. This isn't always possible, but it's likely that you have several art pieces framed in a complementary finish.

4. You can extend furniture up and out on both sides if you have enough art—kind of like a "double-wide." If you need it and it works, do it!

5. The most important rule of all is to keep the room connected by hanging art close to the furniture.

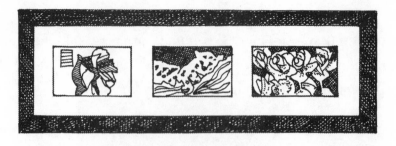

ENHANCE A FIREPLACE.

This is an example of amplifying an architectural feature.

1. Keep the bottom edge of the art connected to (or even with) the lines of the fireplace mantel. This serves to anchor the art to the fireplace feature.

2. Identify the shape of the wall space above the mantel.

3. Most often, a fireplace is the architectural focal point of the room. Strong in lines and material, the fireplace has great impact, and

your goal is to strengthen it. Re-create that sense of weight and strength with art by not only calling attention to the fireplace but dramatizing its impact.

4. Whenever there's an angled ceiling line, such as pitched or cathedral, above the fireplace, you must take it into consideration. The illustration shows how you can connect art to the lines of both the fireplace and the ceiling.

5. Remember, creating the shapes you need can be accomplished with a single piece of art or with multiples, as long as you connect, extend, and enhance what you're working with.

**AMPLIFY AN ARCHITECTURAL SPACE.**
Here you're addressing the architectural space of a pitched wall.

1. Where the ceiling rises, so should the art.

2. Keep the edges of your frames even or anchored on the bottom. Everything in Visual Coordinations is weighted at the bottom and gets lighter as it goes up. This rule also applies to cathedral and step-up walls.

3. Multiple art can be used to create the same overall shapes and lines.

4. Remember: size, shape, and lines. Match them and follow them.

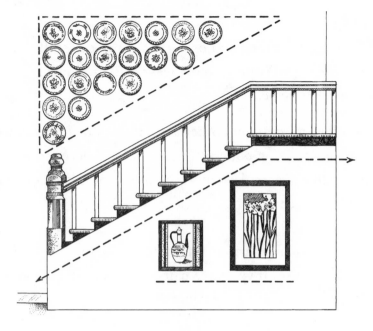

**USE ART ON ODD WALL SHAPES, BOTH LARGE AND SMALL.**
There are two important lessons in this illustration. On the smaller front wall of the staircase, the guidelines are identical to the pitched wall, only condensed.

1.  Where the wall rises, so should the art.

2.  Connect bottom edges to the floor lines, and duplicate the upper lines of the wall as well.

3.  Combinations are always an option, providing you amplify the overall shape.

4.  Now for the back wall of the staircase. You can see in the illustration that the larger back wall forms a perfect triangle. Why not enhance that instead of hanging art randomly up the stair wall? Random art reflects confusion.

USE ART IN CORNERS.

Since I have been warning you over and over not to stuff things into a corner just because it's there, I now want to share some great ideas for using those neglected corners.

1. What I love most about corner art is that it creates an illusion of depth, an intriguing point of interest, and an accent of color in an unexpected place. It also embraces and helps to soften the harsh lines of a corner.

2. The secret to corner art is to use frames that are identical in size, shape, and finish. If you have pairs or sets of art, take another look at the corners in your room.

3. Hang the first two pieces of art the same distance away from the corner wall line, making sure they line up perfectly along the bottom and top edges.

4. With a set of art, you may extend further to broaden the expanse.

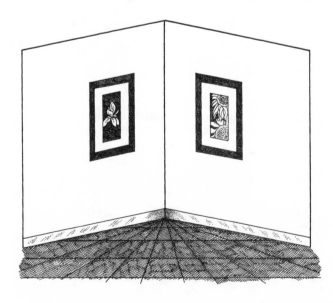

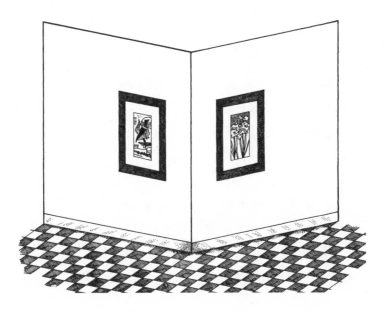

**USE ART WRAPPED AROUND THE CORNER.**
Wraparound art follows the same guidelines as corner art, only you wrap it around the outside corner. Wraparound art works beautifully when it starts in one room and continues into a hallway or other area. It helps to marry seemingly separate areas. Both corner and wraparound art are a real boon to plate collectors.

1. All frames must be identical in size, shape, and finish.

2. Always place the first two pieces the same distance from the outside corner edge of the wall, keeping them even in height.

3. With multiples or a set, you can continue the wraparound display as far as you wish.

CREATE A COLUMN.

1. Use column art wherever you want to create a vertical separation of space. Say, for example, you live in a studio apartment with a tiny dining area that is part of the living room. It needs more definition. Enter column art. It's very adept at creating the illusion of definition or separation.

2. Column art is also great for that tall, skinny wall that tempts you to pop something—anything—on it because, well, it's there, and you hope that one little picture will make it look more important. Instead, you can make that wall taller and more handsome with column art.

3. Simply take art and run it vertically up the wall, keeping the pieces in line and the same distance apart.

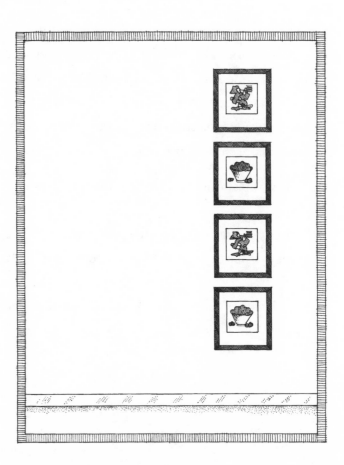

CREATE A CHAIR RAIL.

Creating a chair rail with art forces you to keep sets together instead of scattering them about your home. As you can see, the chair rail technique actually creates an architectural feature.

1. All frames must be identical in size, shape, and finish. This is another technique that works well for plate collectors.

2. Chair-rail art can be used in many ways: to underline a row of windows; to allow tiny frames to emerge from under a lamp shade; to display collector plates in the dining room and eat-in kitchen. I'm sure you'll think of others.

CREATE A GALLERY.

1.  Gallery art is a wonderful way to form an art "field" of any size for a given space. And it allows you to use a combination of different sizes and shapes.

2.  If you don't have one large piece of art, you can now create one.

3.  Gallery art creates a sense of order so you can showcase a theme or a collection.

4.  Gallery art adds movement, interest, and dimension to a room. It's a great device for displaying a potpourri of family treasures. Not surprisingly, the gallery often ends up being a favorite gathering place for family members.

## STEP ONE

LINE UP EVENLY ON TOP EDGE

EVEN ON
SIDE EDGES

LINE UP EVENLY ON BOTTOM EDGE... THEN FILL IN MIDDLE

# STEP TWO

5. Once you decide on the overall size and shape you want, lay the art out on the floor or on a table first. You'll then know the contents of the finished grouping.

6. Follow the directions in the illustration to form the outer edges. The inside space can be filled with anything you want. You could use baskets, hats, dried flowers, wreaths, plates, photos—whatever you want to display.

## STEP THREE

## YOU CAN CREATE ANY SIZE OR SHAPE YOU NEED WITH A GALLERY GROUPING

7.  To secure your gallery art so it doesn't shift every time someone walks by or closes a door, use wall-mount tape—a thin strip of foam with a gentle adhesive on both sides. Put a small strip on the back of the bottom corners, and the artwork will stay in place. Wall-mount tape is available in hardware and craft stores.

1. Hang a mirror across from a window to reflect the natural light or the view; in a foyer, where it serves a function; or above furniture such as a dresser or vanity. I will stretch these rules as far as the end of a hallway, where a mirror can open up a long, narrow space.

2.  Never hang a mirror above the fireplace. In that position, the mirror reflects nothing except the lines of the ceiling directly across from it. The above-the-fireplace mirror is too high and adds absolutely no color, dimension, or interest. It is a tradition completely devoid of design value. (In the past, the mirror may have reflected the light of candles on the mantel, giving the room some needed extra light.)

3.  Mirrors should have a calming effect, not a confusing one. If you have fallen into the trap of mirroring a wall, you probably have a story about of the guest who got up from a chair and walked directly into the mirror. This happens so often when a mirror is not positioned according to the rules of Visual Coordinations. Walls mirrored incorrectly—as on the wrong wall— set up a room of confusion, and even danger.

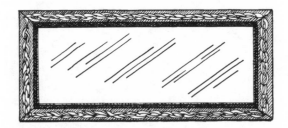

# 6

# Layering the Accessories

We now reach the final stage of Visual Coordinations.
I especially love this part of the formula because accessories are where the true personality of each household
is revealed. It's the little things in a home that can raise it
to a new level of beauty. I find it
interesting that accessories cap-
ture the essence of the homeowner so much
more than do
other
furnishings.

## THE WARM-UP

Since accessories are small, they're an easier and less momentous purchase than a large piece of furniture. We tend to be more impulsive when buying them. It's easier to let the real you come out when cost is not the major consideration. Often accessories are bought during the good times in our lives, or the times when we need to feel better about ourselves. That special item may represent a milestone, a reward, or a weekend getaway. Individual accessories may turn into collections, show your whimsical side, reveal your secret passions, and open the door to your personality. One of the central philosophies to my design formula is that freedom allows beauty and creativity to flower in full. If you really want to discover someone's taste, look at the little things he or she treasures the most.

The best part of layering accessories is that by the time you reach this step, everything else in your room looks good and feels better—including you. The finish line is always the most exciting place to be, and that's where you are now, with the promise of pride, comfort, and beauty as your medal. In this chapter, you'll be introduced to the guidelines for layering accessories. Allow them to lead you, just as they did with furniture and art. And remember that you already grouped your accessories when breaking down your room, so this step will be a lot easier than you think.

### CHANGING LIVES BY DESIGN

*"Imagine being able to change the way people
live in their homes, leaving them with the gift of beauty,
comfort, motivation and renewal, simply by rearranging
the contents that already exist in their households."*

—CAROLE TALBOTT

## TIPS FOR LAYERING THE ACCESSORIES

1. Continue to build peaks and valleys, volume and pause with accessories. Large peaks are constructed with furniture and art; miniature peaks are constructed with the layering of accessories.

2. Keep large with large, small with small, tall with tall, short with short. For example, if you're working with a large, weighty piece of furniture, place strong, weighty accessories on it. Delicate porcelain or crystal would look out of place.

3. China and display cabinets, including bookcases and shelves, should have the larger pieces on the bottom shelves and the smaller, lighter pieces on the top. As with our focus tree, weight starts at the bottom and diminishes as we move up.

4. Cluster accessories that are alike in theme, substance, or color. This establishes consistency and creates pockets of color. Some examples of accessory groupings are pottery, crystal, silver, brass, framed photos, and candlesticks.

5. Don't separate the pieces in pairs, sets, or collections. Items designed to be together should stay together; by separating a collection, you're starting the hunt all over again. Spreading a collection around your home does not make it look like more. Togetherness keeps the collection intact and creates a much greater impact.

6. There is no such thing as good or bad in accessories. If you like something, then it's good for you.

7. Use family photos as accessories in your living room. As a very close part of you, photos should be included in your decorating plans.

8. If money, color, and the number of accessories are limited, you can use common household items to create the effect you want. The list is endless and includes books, magazines, candles, shawls, tablecloths, fabric remnants, yard cuttings, dishes, fresh fruit, children's art, frames, baskets, and hats.

9. While lamps are placed in the furniture step, their shape is determined by their base. For maximum impact, place lamps on tables of similar shape, such as a round-base lamp on a round table.

# VISUAL COORDINATIONS GUIDELINES
# FOR PLACING ACCESSORIES

### COFFEE TABLE

As the heart of every living or family room, the coffee table is where you need a pulse. It is also the place where a quick fix is sure to be noticed. In order to achieve the attention-getting look, reach up into the stagnant space that lurks above all coffee tables. Placing a vertical or tall accessory on it to form a peak (within the guidelines as shown) will easily accomplish this.

Always dress the coffee table first, while you have a wide array of accessories from which to choose. Since the coffee table is so central to the room and will be closely inspected by any visitors, you'll want to show off your finest collection. The coffee table is a good place to practice forming peaks and valleys; on it you can display virtually any treasured piece, from sculptures and flower arrangements to miniature figurines or ashtrays. As I mentioned, you want to extend the low, open space of the coffee table upward by placing tall objects first. From these, you can arrange your peaks and valleys.

Don't worry that flowers on the coffee table might obstruct your view of the television set or a conversation partner across the room. If you were able to put the object on the table, you'll be able to move it away or push it to the side when the television set is on. And besides, do you really want to miss the opportunity of having such a dramatic cen-terpiece in your living room area just because you watch television sometimes?

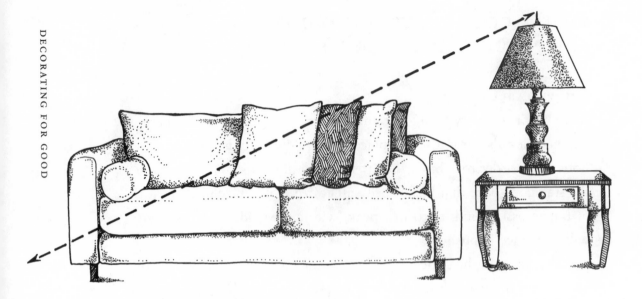

THROW PILLOWS.

Throw pillows might seem too insignificant to make a difference to the overall look of a room, but do not underestimate their worth. Pillows add texture to the flat surface of a couch, fill in hollow corners, and help to emphasize the fluid motion of peaks and valleys.

Look at the end of your sofa nearest the highest lamp—this is the peak end of the sofa. As you know, every peak has descending sides. Since pillows add weight to the sofa, you want to connect them to the high side, allowing the far side to fade away.

Chances are that your throw pillows are currently separated, as in one pillow on the right end of the sofa, another on the left end. This classic arrangement is not only stiff and overly formal; it doesn't look beautiful. Just because this is the way most furniture stores display their sofas, doesn't mean that it works well with the harmony of the room. Clustering all of your pillows toward one end or the other (depending on which side has the peak) will add instant weight and volume, which in turn makes the sofa look cozy and inviting.

## FIREPLACE MANTEL

As with a coffee table, a mantel is a good place to practice achieving a strong peak. An eye-catching architectural detail, the mantelpiece will be admired by your guests, so you want to highlight its features and lines. Unlike the coffee table, though, it offers only a long, narrow space, so you're limited in the kind of objects you can place there. Also, mantels are much closer to eye level than are coffee tables, so you should be conscious of the angle at which admirers will be viewing your pieces.

Accessories such as candlesticks, small plants, miniature objects, boxes, figurines, and leather-bound books make for a nice display. People often make the mistake of separating pairs of candlesticks or matching vases by placing one on either end of the mantel. This sets up a separation zone and creates a rigid display instead of one that is free-flowing and natural. To me this seems too symmetrical and coldly correct—which is ironic, considering the display is over a warm fire. First and foremost, your home and accessories should feel comfortable and inviting.

To ensure an eye-catching display, cluster like items together according to color, finish, and theme wherever possible.

## TABLETOPS

By now it should be obvious that all accessories follow the same basic peak-to-valley guidelines. Maintaining the up-and-down movement throughout the room is vital to the renewed pulse of your living space.

It's also important to remember to place like or similar objects with one another. As you learned, this applies to clustering pairs, but it also refers to placing accessories on a table of a particular shape. When positioning round or oval accessories, consider putting them on a round tabletop. The same principle applies to a square or rectangular table. In that way the accessories echo the basic shape of the furniture, and the overall form is emphasized.

SHELVES, BOOKCASES, DISPLAY CABINETS,
ARCHITECTURAL LEDGES

Once again, the same guidelines apply: establish peak-to-valley movement; cluster like accessories; keep weighty pieces on lower shelves.
Think of the weight at the base of a mountain, and build the same
sense of weight at the base of shelves, bookcases, and display cabinets.

If your bookcase is true to its name and holds nothing but books,
continue to apply the placement technique—keep the biggest books on
the bottom and the smallest on top.

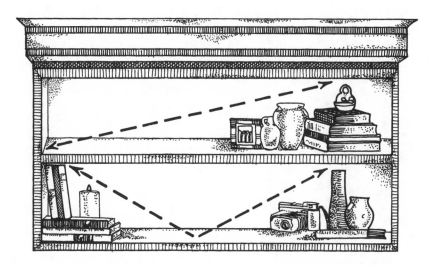

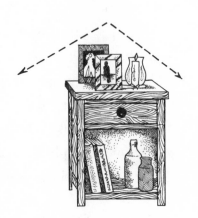

## EXTENDING FURNITURE WITH ACCESSORIES

It's important to be aware of the size and shape of the furniture you're working with. Certainly a small table looks overwhelmed when it is topped with a large, heavy accessory, just as a massive piece of furniture looks out of balance with one or even several small and delicate accessories.

The objective is to make tall taller, small smaller, heavy heavier, and light lighter. In other words, continue the motion that your furniture begins, because the furniture is tied to the architecture, and that is the basis for the formula.

### DINING ROOM TABLES

Don't ignore the dining room table when it is time to accessorize—it won't be set for a meal at all times. Think of it as an oversize tabletop, and continue to accent the size. A teacup of flowers in the center of a dining room table does not work. Instead, give it the weight and height it deserves. If the table is rectangular, duplicate that shape in your accessory. Ditto with round, oval, or square tables. Displays substantial in size add drama and can be easily removed for dining.

## HOUSEPLANTS

My edict is *No hanging plants inside the home.* According to our formula, everything we arrange is anchored at the bottom (from the floor up) to provide a solid foundation of furniture, art, and accessories. Every piece is also connected or related to every other. As we arrange upward and outward, things get lighter.

Plants are anchored, either in the ground or on a tree, and in trying to replicate the natural order inside the home, it doesn't make sense to hang them from the ceiling or window frame. Plants should be connected to the floor, to a piece of furniture, or to a ledge. That is where they look better, feel better, and grow better. If you must hang plants, try to do so in a garden room or greenhouse, but never in the main part of the house.

If you have a number of houseplants, cluster them to create lush "pocket gardens." Don't spread them throughout the house. In nature, plants do best and look best when they have company; in your home, the grouping will have a much greater impact than would a single plant.

As I mentioned when discussing standing plants, don't shove trees or other large plants into corners just because an empty space exists.

Bring your trees and plants out into the room where they can flourish and be admired. Plants add a feeling of life; when they are stuck in a corner, usually without much sunlight, their color fades and the leaves gather dust. They want to be an integral part of your home, so honor them by putting them in the proper place and connecting them to the beautiful new arrangement of your room. If you don't have any large plants and feel your room needs greenery, gather some branches to place in a large vase to add a note of freshness.

This rule even applies to silk plants and arrangements. I have been in so many homes where every tabletop sprouted an arrangement. The overall effect was diluted by so many little groupings. If you recognize this problem in your own home, gather those arrangements up, take them apart, and build just a few larger, more impressive combinations.

## Looking Back

By this point, your holding area should be back to its original state. If any pieces did not return to the room you've been working on, store them in a closet until you're ready to work on another room.

I hope you have remembered to take photographs throughout the rearranging process, because this is the payoff. Now that you have finished placing the furniture, hanging the art, and layering the accessories, the only thing left to do is to enjoy the results (and, if you are ambitious, gather energy for the next room).

# 7

# The Other Rooms— A Field Trip

Now that you're starting to sprout your wings a bit, let's take a trip to your other rooms and discuss ways to apply what you've learned so far to the foyer, dining room, bedroom, kitchen, bathroom, and even the porch and patio. In each room, we'll discuss the key parts of the Visual Coordinations formula that apply, calling them placement points, and we'll provide you with some great tips to help you put everything in its place.

# FOYER

❖  The architectural focal point is not addressed.
❖  Select furniture that fits the wall space or overall area of your
   foyer.
❖  Layer art to your furniture pieces or wall space.
❖  Accessorize with a major piece or grouping of like items.
❖  Anchor the foyer with an area rug.
❖  Don't forget that mirrors work well in foyers.

Many times foyers are overlooked in spite of their important
function: welcoming your guests. The last thing you want is an area
that feels empty or uninviting. Consider adding a chair (perhaps from
your dining room) if there is enough room. This gives the foyer a sense
of "room." Area rugs add color, weight, and warmth. Don't discount
adding a tree, greenery, or floral arrangements, as they always make a
warm and friendly statement. For an extra-large foyer, placing a table
in the center to create a weaving pattern around its edges sets the stage
for a dramatic impact. Remember: Using all of the space, no matter
how large or small, is the secret to success.

# DINING ROOM

❖  The architectural focal point is not addressed.
❖  Furniture placement is based purely on function in this room.
❖  Consider removing large side pieces (such as a breakfront) to
   another room.
❖  Layer your art to furniture pieces or wall spaces.

❖ Accessory impact can be increased by using a large centerpiece on the dining table.

The dining room tends to be the most crowded room in a home, with limited space for movement. I have found a simple solution to this problem: remove the breakfront! Many times it turns out to be just the tall, weighty piece that's needed in the living room.

Furniture designers take a lot of care in constructing the lines and shapes of dining room suites, but often having a breakfront squeezed along a side wall detracts from the visual impact of not only the dining table but the breakfront as well. Visually, everything runs together, including the chandelier. It takes on the feeling of one big mass (or mess) of furniture with little room for comfort, beauty, or function.

By removing the breakfront, you will lighten up your dining room, and the room that is lucky enough to receive it takes on a note of elegance. After all, what do we display in breakfronts? Our most beautiful and cherished items—which may go totally unnoticed when stuffed in the dining room.

With this newfound space you may find that adding a leaf to the table works beautifully and elegantly. Layer in some favorite art or add a substantial table centerpiece, and you'll feel like *dining* instead of *eating*.

Be careful not to line too many pieces around the dining room walls. This will add confusion and defeat the purpose of the dining experience. Make sure you include a nice long pause between the pieces you have placed. Trees and greenery add to the feeling of comfort.

# KITCHEN

## PLACEMENT POINTS

❖ Architectural focal points are not addressed.

❖ If you have room for a work or breakfast table, make sure it fits the space available.

❖ Kitchen art is great; just follow the wall shape guidelines.

❖ Follow the same accessory guidelines, creating peaks and valleys.

❖ Consider adding a kitchen rug for a real splash of color. There are so many beautiful choices today.

The placement guidelines you'll focus on in your kitchen are the guidelines for art (addressing the shape of your wall space) and accessories (clustering and grouping like things together); be sure not to forget the pause or valley in between.

If your kitchen has a large open space in the center, definitely start scouting for a chopping block or work table. They do not cramp your kitchen style, and they enhance the overall function of the space. I always keep a large bowl of fruit and a canister of biscotti on mine.

Another valuable tip for eat-in areas is that square and rectangular tables work better than round-topped tables. Believe it or not, the round shape actually eats up more space.

# BEDROOM

## PLACEMENT POINTS

❖ Architectural focal points are not addressed in bedrooms.

❖ Place your bed first, according to the largest space available.

❖ Pockets of space are filled with pieces that fit the overall space.

❖ Layer art to furniture and wall space.

❖ The same accessory guidelines apply in bedrooms.

The most-often-asked question regarding bedrooms is "What do I do with the focal point?" Nothing! You don't go into a bedroom to sit in bed and admire the architectural focal point. Placement becomes function in this room. What you do focus on first in the bedroom is placing the bed in the space that accommodates it best—generally near or on the longest wall.

In a very small bedroom, try angling the bed to a corner, as you would a sofa in a small square room, and the same results will occur. There's actually a sense of more space thanks to those pockets.

In a very large bedroom, you can consider floating the bed out into the room, using all of the space, and then layering from there. Consider adding a dresser behind the head of the bed.

Avoid putting a bed in front of a window. Windows are *not* headboards, and doing this will close down the room and reduce the natural light.

Once the bed has been "landed," the formula picks up its old rules. Look at the piece and match it to the space available: large-to-large, small-to-small, counterbalancing the furniture weight as you go. In other words you don't want *all* of your side pieces lined up along one wall. Bedrooms depend on a certain amount of function—with nightstands (his and hers) and reading lamps, for example—but don't forget to create livable areas as well, especially in a large bedroom. Bring in a love seat and a couple of chairs, even a coffee table. This offers you a wonderful private escape.

Layer your art in the same way that you have in all the other rooms, connecting it to furniture or wall space. Mirrors will be placed according to function (attached to a dresser or full-length). The final touch remains a constant: accessories, to which the same guidelines apply.

## BATHROOM

### PLACEMENT POINTS

❖ Architectural focal points are not addressed.

❖ If you have furniture in your bathroom, place it according to the space available.

❖ Art generally follows the guideline of addressing the wall space or is connected to towel bars.

❖ Accessories will be in small groupings, or there may be one large statement piece.

If you want to walk on the wild side of decorating, start in the bathroom. It's the best place to introduce the colors you love but are afraid to use anywhere else. Because you're working on a smaller scale in a bathroom, being adventuresome feels less risky.

Start with the towels and shower curtain, or a piece of art, to set your color scheme and your overall theme. Paint is the last selection you make and should act as the common thread that pulls it all together. If I can paint leopard spots in my powder room, just think what you can do!

Have fun with your art and accessories—anything can be considered a part of this room, as long as *you* like it. Bathrooms are great homes for candles, plants, and general accessory adventure. I've placed large shells in one shower and a beautiful sculpture in another! Once you've experienced this freedom from limitation, your eyes will start roaming over the rest of your house with the same sense of adventure.

# PATIO AND PORCH

## PLACEMENT POINTS

❖ The focal point will be addressed as your starting point.

❖ Furniture guidelines are the same as for living and family rooms.

❖ Less art will be used because there is at most one wall, or on the patio, none.

❖ Accessories—same, same, same.

The trick to patios and porches is to treat them like rooms. Read the overall shape and follow the guidelines for that room shape.

If the porch is attached to the living or family room, continue the tacking pattern from the room into the porch, allowing the two separate spaces to flow together.

Avoid lining furniture up along the house wall so that every seat is looking out. This keeps you from using all of the space and pretty much eliminates conversation.

I have a specific rule of *not* hanging houseplants inside the house (which I discussed in Chapter 7), but you can break this rule in your outdoor rooms. Porches and patios lend themselves to becoming garden rooms, and the plants are happier in these spaces.

By now you must be coming to the realization that this formula can be adapted to any part of your home where there is movable furniture. For those of you with furniture that is built-in, the guidelines you can follow are the ones for art and accessories. I've had many requests to rearrange yachts, which I find rather amusing since everything is either built-in or nailed down. But even in those instances, I can still apply other principles of the Visual Coordinations formula, which is just another way of saying that we can only do what we can do. Happy rearranging, wherever you can.

# 8

# Your Natural Colors: Fabric and Paint

By now you have realized how different your home can look just by rearranging furnishings that you've owned and used for years. Imagine what a dramatic improvement a new coat of paint or some fresh upholstery would make. After experiencing the exhilarating effects of rearranging, you probably have the urge to go one step further. It's hard to stop when you are surrounded by such satisfying results, and adding or changing color is the natural next step.

Since the Visual Coordinations formula follows the lines and motion of nature, it is natural to start there for an education in color. I want you to look at color—and the choices you have—in a new and different way. Right outside your door is a wonderful color wheel, nature's most spectacular gift. Think about the millions of combinations of contrasting and complementary colors in your backyard, the myriad shades of green in a single plant, and the manner by which insects change their coloration for survival. Color affects life so dramatically, yet too often we ignore the grand selection and choose instead to surround ourselves with safe, neutral tones—white, ivory, gray, brown, and black—especially when decorating a home.

Nature gives us a wide choice of color from which to choose, so we have the opportunity to discover what inspires us. This makes color a very personal expression and gives onlookers (or visitors to your home) an insight into your style, taste, and preferences. I believe that if you surround yourself with the colors that attract you instinctively, you will be showing your true self and will feel more comfortable within your environment. This is most important in your home, where you spend time relaxing, reflecting, sharing special moments with family, and hosting friends.

In my opinion, there is no such thing as a bad color—only a wrong color for you. Neutral tones are beautiful and look stylish in many homes, but you should not feel that beige and white are your only decorating options, especially if you're a vivacious risk-taker who loves to wear red. In this case, bold colors probably suit your personality better and make you feel happy. So why not translate that energy into your home? We all have favorite colors and others we cannot tolerate.

So how do you pick the colors that are correct for you? Easy. You can do it instinctively, by choosing colors that attract you without thought. Doing it this way ensures that you will be happy with the outcome and diminishes insecure feelings, like wondering what other people will think or debating whether your choice follows the fashion trend.

The colors you choose (assuming you like them), and the medium—such as upholstery, curtain fabric, paint, wallpaper, or wood stain—on which the color will appear, do not matter. The sequence, however, does. When changing or adding color, you should select fabrics first and paint last.

## Selecting Fabric

Keep in mind that I'm teaching you this technique not to be different, but because it works without fail every time. So head to the nearest fabric center and imagine that you are a child in the best toy store in town. You wouldn't think about which toys are practical, inexpensive, or durable, so don't labor over finding the "right" fabric. Let your instincts lead you to the one that you absolutely love.

1. Walk slowly through the fabric center, browsing until you find the fabric that pulls you the strongest. Don't think about whether it will go with the colors at home, where you will use it, or even how much it costs. All that matters is that you love it. This is a new day, and a new way of making choices, with the freedom to be who you are. The first fabric is the most important choice you'll make, because the real you made it. It is your personal fabric; use it to guide you the rest of the way. When I finish this exercise in my training seminars, almost all the students return from their shopping trip surprised at their selection, pointing out that they would never have been able to do this before. And I even have a secret (which I will share later) for simply looking at the fabric that someone has chosen and knowing if he or she cheated.

2. With a sample of your favorite fabric in hand, go back to the field to select your next one. Go with your instinct again, but this time there are a few restrictions. The second fabric must complement the first one in color and contrast with it in pattern. By that I mean that if the first pattern is rounded or free-flowing, the second pattern should be linear or geometric. Don't worry; once you have the first fabric to guide you, choosing others will be very easy.

3. With two fabrics in hand, go back and select the third and final one. This should be a solid in a color that serves as a bridge to bring the first two fabrics together. (Although I said solid, the fabric can also be tone-on-tone, heavy weave, or nubby, as long as the overall effect is that of a solid color.)

*Note:* The selection process of patterned and solid fabrics can vary in sequence, providing you end up with a free-flowing rounded pattern, a linear, geometric pattern, and a solid.

In every fabric center I have ever visited, clerks tell me how hard it is for many customers to find the right fabric. It takes most shoppers days—sometimes weeks—before they're ready to commit to a fabric. Even then, they may still leave with a feeling of uncertainty. In contrast, clerks love to see my students walk in the door because they know exactly what kind of fabric they're looking for. The formula teaches them how to approach the fabric dilemma, saves them lots of time, and lets them leave

the store feeling confident. Now you can do the same thing—just try it. And remember that the staff at the fabric center is there to help you with the measurements.

One other thing: If you happen to select a really expensive fabric that will ruin your budget, don't get discouraged. You can still have it in your home by using it as an accent, such as for a throw pillow or an end table covering, rather than covering a couch or chair. You won't need much yardage for that.

Back to the secret of how I can tell when someone has cheated in the fabric selection process: If you take the first fabric you selected (you know, the one that represents the real you), go to a mirror, and wrap the fabric around your shoulders, you should feel wonderful. Watch what happens to your eyes, your skin tone, even your hair color. Suddenly you take on a radiance, just as your room will. That is what I look for when my students return from their shopping trip. If I do not see it, I know that the student probably got confused or felt insecure and just chose the first fabric he or she saw. Trust your instincts. They will guide you correctly if you let them.

## Selecting Paint

Because the Visual Coordinations formula changes the mood of the room, it is wise to select paint color after you have completed the rearranging process. Look at the room you just rearranged. Is there a different color or shade that now predominates? Consider the furniture you may have bought, the curtains you may have installed, or the new upholstery you may have added. This transformation of the room plays a big part in the final decision on paint color because the room itself becomes your partner in choosing a color that suits both of you. Focusing on the room makes the decision so much easier.

In choosing a paint color, keep in mind that light colors will reflect light and visually expand the room, while dark colors will absorb the light, making the space feel closer. Think about the purpose of your rooms, how you use them, what time of day you use them, and what the natural and artificial light sources are. Along with the furnishings, these variables should play a role in the colors you choose. For instance, a room in which you eat breakfast and spend the morning might feel best in a light or bright shade—the color acting as a wake-up signal. Conversely, a small den in which you read, pay bills, or chat with a friend over coffee might feel coziest in a dark shade—the color wrapping you like a warm blanket.

If you have finished rearranging your belongings but still feel that the room is missing something, chances are the color scheme needs a little help. Color can be fun, especially when it is used properly to accent your furnishings and represent your personal style. Approach it with this attitude and remember to follow your instincts—you will be surprised at how creative and unique you can be.

# 9

# Taking the Formula Outdoors: Landscaping

If you can enhance the interior architecture with a placement technique, why can't you do the same on the outside? While many people spend hours making certain that their living space is harmonious and beautiful, they often forget that the outside of the home, especially the front facade, is the true reflection of one's personality. There is no need to dig up your yard or to hire a team of landscape architects, though. With a slight variation to the Visual Coordinations formula, you can achieve the same successful results outside your home. Let's take a walk outdoors and discover a simple new way to make landscaping work for you.

When you drive down a residential street, glancing at each home as you pass, chances are that some of the houses catch your eye while others, even though they may be expensive, well built, or situated on a nice lot, just don't look as good. Of course everyone likes different architectural styles, but my guess is that the homes that immediately attract you have one thing in common: the landscape is in alignment with the architecture.

The importance of balancing the architectural lines and shapes (the constant) with the surrounding elements (the variables) has already been proven by your work inside the home. Now you can apply that knowledge to the facade of your home, the first (and maybe only) feature of your home life that passers-by may see.

The basic definition of landscaping is "to improve the grounds around a building." There is no mention of extending, enhancing, or relating the plants to the building, and one could conclude that the building and the grounds are completely separate. You, of course, know better than that by now. The building is connected to the grounds and must be treated as such. Landscaping gives you the perfect opportunity to enhance what you already have and to add natural order, literally, to your life. In addition, matching plant shapes to architectural shapes is a fun project for all you weekend gardeners and new homeowners.

Remember the Imperial Gardens of Beijing, and how the emperors made sure that the gardens were connected to—and partially obscured —the buildings? In this way the two became one, flowing together naturally. The height and mass of the plantings were carefully considered before they were anchored to the buildings. The gardens create a lasting impression, and the visitor departs with a wonderful feeling of peace and comfort. By following the placement formula outside, you can bring those ancient principles to your own home. The rules for the exterior of your home are identical to those for the interior.

# Landscaping Tips

- ❖ Visually divide the exterior walls of your home into sections, or different wall shapes, and then address each one individually. Refer back to the wall shapes in Chapter 3 if you need to refresh your memory.

- ❖ Like furniture, art, and accessories, plants and trees are the pieces on the puzzle board; place them accordingly. Where the roofline rises, so should the plantings. Plant tall where the roofline is high, and short where the roofline is low. If the line moves straight across, maintain that line in shrubbery.

- ❖ Think of height and weight as motion and pause. Layer other plants to the tallest, bringing them out into the lawn or yard to create height and depth at the same time.

- ❖ Tall-taller translates to strong-stronger. The weighty sections of architecture are where the weighty plants are placed. Simply add to what you already have.

- ❖ If you cannot afford to buy the height you need, buy plants that will eventually grow to it. It's fun to watch your plants and your home gradually complement one another.

- ❖ Large trees are obviously difficult—if not impossible—to move. So if they do not exactly fit the formula, we must work with them or around them.

- ❖ Take your interior theme into consideration. For example, if your home is traditional in style, continue that feeling in your landscaping. Leafy, soft, loose foliage complements traditional architecture. If your home is contemporary, straight-edged, strong, geometric plantings work best. Always continue with the basic theme that has already been established.

- ❖ With all the colors that nature provides, there's no problem finding flowering plants that connect with the colors inside your home.

For example, in my home I use a profusion of red and gold, so when I visit the garden center, I always head to the section that displays flowering plants of those colors.

❖ When shopping for trees and plants, ask about the growth rate. When I moved into my present home, I wanted plants that grew fast and full. I also wanted plants I could trim and shape, creating varying heights and volume to enhance the exterior architecture.

❖ Of course the availability of plants and trees will vary depending on where you live. Although selections vary from one part of the country to another, you can always find the shapes and sizes you need to enhance the exterior of your home.

❖ Applying the placement technique to the exterior of your home can be done all at once or a little at a time. If you work a little at a time, you can use the interim periods to plot your next landscaping move.

❖ Most planting can be done by you and your family. When planting trees, however, it is prudent to call your garden center or lawn care company for help.

❖ Consider the growing conditions for plants when placing them. If you don't have the proper soil, water, or sunlight conditions for a particular plant, try to find a similar-looking one that will thrive in the space.

Now that I have spent time with you in your home, I'd like to invite you to mine. Because I have used the exterior of my home as a basis for much of my experimenting with landscaping, I want to share the results with you. Here you can see the formula in action. Let's start with the exterior architecture, first reviewing it as a whole and then breaking it down into wall and roofline sections.

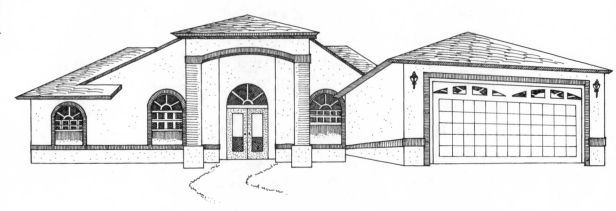

# The Whole House

This drawing shows the architectural features of the house and the lines around which I will place plants and trees. To the left is the low side (valley) of the roofline. As we move to the right, the roof starts to rise (peak), moving not only up but also out into the front lawn. Past the midsection, the roofline begins to decline into another valley. The right side of the house has a lower roofline that comes forward into the front lawn, while at the same time creating a flat wall.

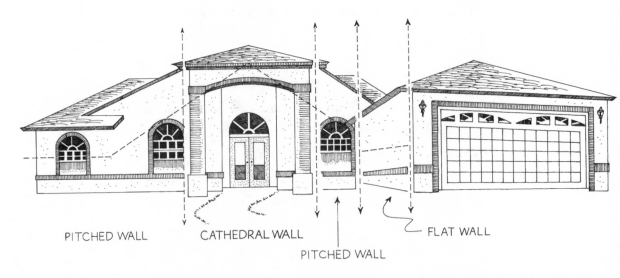

PITCHED WALL          CATHEDRAL WALL          FLAT WALL

PITCHED WALL

You can see how we break down the architecture into manageable sections for planting.

Now that we have identified and divided the exterior architecture, let's go back and draw in the layer of landscaping in each section.

Where the roofline is lowest, the plants are lowest. The hedge starts to gradually rise, following the rising roofline. As you can see, we are duplicating the architectural lines, enhancing or extending the home with landscaping while connecting the two.

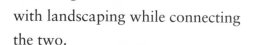

As the roofline reaches its peak in the center section, so do the plants and trees. In addition I have added or layered plants to reach out into the front lawn because this is the weighty section of the house. Remember our rule: Make big bigger, heavy heavier, tall taller, short shorter.

As the roofline starts to descend at the right, so do the plants in the garden.

This section extends out into the lawn with a long, flat wall. Here I have built a long, horizontal garden with a birdbath. For variation or movement, a short flowering tree is connected to the birdbath, creating a small peak away from the wall. Remember, the flat wall is the only shape that allows you to choose where you want to establish a peak. The projecting corner of the flat wall is softened with a small cluster of vertical evergreens, just as you might do with wraparound art on the interior.

The influence of art can also be seen in the double-door front entrance. I keep wreaths on the doors year-round, changing them with the seasons. It's important that both doors are decorated equally. During drives through my neighborhood, I'm always surprised — and dismayed — to see a double-door entrance with a wreath on only one

door. Please take note: two doors, two wreaths. This is another rule designed to enhance, rather than ignore, the architecture.

The Visual Coordinations concept begins in nature, and it returns to nature time and time again. We have taken a leisurely walk along an enticing new path of home decorating, learning a great deal as we wend our way through the twists and turns, the peaks and valleys— only to discover that it is the simple solutions that work best. I hope you enjoy applying the formula to your home and your life. You are sure to see—and feel—wonderful results.

# 10
## The Visual Reality, in Conclusion

While this book is designed to guide you in rearranging the main living quarters of your home, the Visual Coordinations formula extends well beyond the living room, family room, or den. You are more likely to make a change in a room that friends and family share, but there is no rule that you must start or stop there. If you are already comfortable with the arrangement in your living area, apply the tips you have learned to other rooms of your home. If, on the other hand, you used the technique to transform your living room, you now see how amazing the results can be. So apply the formula to the bedroom, kitchen, bathroom, office, or patio, and don't forget the landscaping.

Now that you know what each step of the placement technique entails, the process will be much faster and easier. You will be able to redecorate any room of your house by following the same guidelines. Remember to read the architecture and align the furniture with the shape of the room, hang art according to the architecture and the placement of the furniture, and then add the accessories. Just keep in mind the basic checkpoints—peaks and valleys, weaving traffic patterns, diagonal and triangular light patterns—and you'll do fine.

In conclusion, this book is about feeling good about yourself and your surroundings. That alone provides you with a sense of comfort you may not have experienced until now. Puff up and be proud; this is your home. With comfort and pride come other pleasing emotions such as the removal of the fear of being judged in your home, and the confusion of adding additional purchases becomes a thing of the past.

Here are the emotional checkpoints of Visual Coordinations, all of which I'm sure you're already enjoying.

❖ You now have the look of beauty and the feeling of comfort.

❖ The motivation to go further and a newfound confidence to open your home more freely to others is empowering to say the least.

❖ Most important of all, you have renewed the sense of pride in your home.

Having beauty and comfort in one's home is a right everyone deserves, whether you live in a mobile home or that mansion on a hill. Up until now the only piece that has been missing from the design puzzle is the final one, how to fit it all together. Visual Coordinations is not only the final piece—it is the final peace!

Because you now have a taste of how simple it is to transform your home, enhance what you own, and amplify who you are, I'd like to close with a few stories of actual clients with whom I have worked. These people, just like you maybe, were a little fearful of trying to redecorate their home themselves, confused about how rearranging furnishings could make a difference, and worried that the placement techniques would not work in their home. Well, miracles do happen. I'm reminded of this power again and again as I go into homes to do my job. Hopefully you'll identify with the following examples and have a new appreciation of the outcome. Each of my thousands of clients, even those who have failed with other decorating methods, sees results with Visual Coordinations, as you have.

Some years ago, I worked in a home that had recently been put up for sale. Two doctors were getting divorced and decided to try Visual Coordination in the hopes of improving the home's interior for a quick sale. As soon as I entered the house, I sensed separation. Although there were many beautiful pieces of art from their world travels, it lacked a feeling of connection or comfort. It was clear to me that the home was arranged in a way that exerted a negative influence on the lives of its owners. There was no place for the couple to be themselves, to relax and share moments together. They could not spend quality time together in their busy professional lives, and unfortunately, they could not do so at home either.

I worked with the housekeeper in rearranging the furnishings; as we worked through the steps, her emotional distress over the pending upheaval waned, and she became much calmer. When the doctors returned to survey the results, they mirrored her reaction, exclaiming how much the room looked like them. Two weeks later, I received a call from a disgruntled realtor informing me the sale was off. The couple had decided not to sell after all—and not to divorce.

Two devoted sons asked me to work in the home of their recently widowed father. He was having problems adjusting to the death of his wife, refusing to let his sons move any of her things, yet unable to cope with the constant reminders of happier times. The sons were afraid the surroundings would make the mourning process more difficult and prolonged. They took their father away for the day while I came in and rearranged. When they all returned and saw the change, the father broke down and wept. He told me that his home now felt so different, yet his wife's things were still there. Several weeks later one son called to thank me "for saving my father's life." He was still grieving, of course, but in a much more constructive way.

The home of a recently retired "power" couple tells a different story. Reflecting their strong and successful personalities, and filled with treasures collected over a lifetime, their new home in Florida had not achieved the same comfort level as their previous home in Connecticut. They kept finding excuses to get away from it—shopping, golfing, dining out, anything to delay going home.

After I worked on it using the Visual Coordination system, they marveled at the dramatic change. They were surprised at how the furniture was placed in areas they never would have thought of trying and thought it gave the home a welcoming feeling. For the first time, they were able to relax and really enjoy their retirement.

Visual Coordinations works for children as well as adults, and since many households include kids, it is a useful tool. One of my clients had a five-year old son who was an absolute terror and loved to rip the house to shreds. His poor mother was desperate for some peace and order, so approached Visual Coordinations.

As I was completing the process, I dreaded the consequences, assured that the child would destroy all the work I had done. When mother and son returned home, I was not surprised by the look of amazement and joy on her face, but I was stunned by her son's reaction. He entered the room cautiously, sat down politely, and closely looked around at all the furnishings. The change on his personality was immediate, and I later discovered that the effect was lasting. He became quite neat with his room, wanting it to look like the rest of the house.

Visual Coordination not only settled the home, but it settled the little boy and brought him a sense of respect and care for his belongings. This incident made me realize that when a house is in chaos, everyone who lives there is, too. And, if parents do not take pride in their home, neither will their children.

These are only a few of the stories that prove how useful and effective the system can be, not only for bringing out the natural beauty of a home, but for changing people's lives. While I can't guarantee that Visual Coordinations will save your marriage or calm your children, it will bring beauty, order, and balance to your home and thus, your life.

# Visual Coordinations For the Professional

Visual Coordinations is not just for the frustrated home-maker, but for the professional designer as well. Since interior design is a service business, Visual Coordinations is a perfect fit. And because the VC formula has a purely scientific base, the learning process is a simple one.

There are many people out there who really do have a knack for decorating, and have no idea how to go about turning it into earning power. The time and cost of formal training are usually not an option. But enrolling in a five-day certifica-tion program in Visual Coordinations is. The program offers the creative person a great opportunity to work for his- or herself, and to help others. (See resource page 160.)

For experienced interior designers, Visual Coordinations adds an exciting new layer to their education while rekindling their creativity and expanding their ability to serve clients. It also enables the designer to immediately identify the client's taste in order to enhance it, not change it. We have found that by integrating Visual Coordinations into a design business, sales increase. This happens because the designer works with household treasures before recommending new purchases, thereby gaining the confidence of the client. By applying the VC formula, the designer knows exactly what to add and where to place it. The guessing game is stopped dead in its tracks. And the homemaker stays connected to the project throughout.

Even architects can benefit. Addressing the placement of interior pieces not only enhances and amplifies their work but takes a lot of the pressure off the design and move-in process. How often is the architect blamed for designing a space that turns out to be unrelated to the art of living? Visual Coordinations can bridge the gap between structure and interior design.

## The Gift of Visual Coordination

Most gratifying of all, visual coordination can be used to help others in need. More and more of us are discovering that giving a gift that improves the way we live and changes the way we feel about ourselves and others is very empowering. What better starting point to changing the world than changing our home?

# Resources

Carole Talbott is an accomplished motivational and educational speaker. In addition to her ongoing work with the interior design industry, she offers Visual Coordinations Certification Training to those who want to offer these services professionally, and has developed educational products to instruct homemakers in applying the Visual Coordination process to their own homes.

Ms. Talbott is also available for personal interviews, speaking engagements, guest appearances, product information, and for scheduling training seminars. For assistance in locating a Visual Coordinator in your local area, please contact the Visual Coordination corporate office.

E-MAIL   carole@ctalbott.com
PHONE    (561) 220–8144
FAX      (561) 220-2326
MAIL     P.O. Drawer 467
         Port Salerno, FL 34992–0467

Or visit the Visual Coordination website at www.ctalbott.com